ADVANCED WITCHCRAFT

EXPLORING DEEPER LEVELS OF SPIRITUAL SKILLS AND MASTERFUL MAGIC

About the Author

PATRICIA TELESCO (TRISH) has been a part of the Neo-Pagan community for over 30 years. During that time, she penned many memorable titles, including *Victorian Grimoire, Goddess in my Pocket, Spinning Spells; Weaving Wonders,* and the first edition of *Kitchen Witch's Cookbook.*

ADVANCED WITCHCRAFT

EXPLORING DEEPER LEVELS OF SPIRITUAL SKILLS AND MASTERFUL MAGIC

PATRICIA TELESCO

Chicago, Illinois

Advanced Witchcraft: Exploring Deeper Levels of Masterful Magic © 2025 by Crossed Crow Books. All rights reserved. No part of this book may be reproduced in any manner whatsoever without written permission from Crossed Crow Books, except in the case of brief quotations embodied in critical articles and reviews.

Paperback ISBN: 978-1-964537-06-1
Hardcover ISBN: 978-1-964537-40-5
Library of Congress Control Number on file.

Disclaimer: Crossed Crow Books, LLC does not participate in, endorse, or have any authority or responsibility concerning private business transactions between our authors and the public. Any internet references contained in this work were found to be valid during the time of publication, however, the publisher cannot guarantee that a specific reference will continue to be maintained. This book's material is not intended to diagnose, treat, cure, or prevent any disease, disorder, ailment, or any physical or psychological condition. The author, publisher, and its associates shall not be held liable for the reader's choices when approaching this book's material. The views and opinions expressed within this book are those of the author alone and do not necessarily reflect the views and opinions of the publisher.

Published by:
Crossed Crow Books, LLC
6934 N Glenwood Ave, Suite C
Chicago, IL 60626
www.crossedcrowbooks.com

Printed in the United States of America.
IBI

Acknowledgments

I would like to gratefully acknowledges the many elders in the Wiccan community who took the time to share insights, exercises, and advice for the pages of this book.

Special thanks go to Colleen, Dorothy, Arawn, Robin, Frank and Cate, A. J., Jennie, Steven, the folks at WADL, Michael, Kym, and Sirona, all of whom have inspired me by their dedication to sharing the truth in love and wisdom.

For all these people, and everyone who walks the Path of Beauty with sincerity as a guide, may the God and Goddess smile upon you and bless you now and always.

CONTENTS

Author's Note to the Novice xi

INTRODUCTION • 1

Note from the Author 4

Chapter One
DEFINING THE ADEPT • 5

Archetypes of Adepthood 6
The Leap of Faith 10
Making a Commitment 17
Dedication Ritual 18
Living the Magic 23
What to Expect Along the Way 25

Chapter Two
A MOMENT'S PAUSE • 28

Recognition 29
Integration and Expression 35
Motivation 41
Advanced Witchcraft: The Human Factor 44

Chapter Three
DYNAMIC TRADITIONAL MAGIC • 45

Pets as Familiars 50
Spells, Charms, and Amulets 53

Chapter Four
MAGICAL ARTISTRY • 73

Magical Muse 76
Mazes and Labyrinths 85
Glamoury 87

Chapter Five
DREAMWORK • 94

The Dream Diary. 95
The Sacred Sleep Space 97
Personal Dreamtime Magic 100
Lucid Dreaming 101
Programmed Dreaming 103
Divinely Inspired Dreaming. 105
Psychic and Prophetic Dreaming 108

Chapter Six
TRANCEWORK AND PATHWORKING • 112

Trance Work 113
Group Trances. 116
Information Retrieval from Spirit 118
Channeling 120
Prophetic Trances. 122

Pathworking 124
Group Pathworking.................... 133
Vision Quests 138

Chapter Seven
WORKING WITH NATURAL AND ELEMENTAL SPIRITS • 140

Spiritual Safety 141
A Ghost of a Chance................... 142
Necromancy........................... 143
Mediumship 144
Of Nature, Myth, and Magic 147
Legendary Energy..................... 147
Totems and Guides 152
Elemental Spirits...................... 155

Chapter Eight
SERVING THE COMMUNITY • 164

Study Groups......................... 169
Gatherings and Lectures 171
Covens............................... 173
Healing 175
Counseling........................... 177
Monitoring and Regulation 180
Community Magic..................... 182
Self-Care and Maintenance 185

Afterword
THE DIVINE COPILOT • 187

Recommended Reading 189

AUTHOR'S NOTE TO THE NOVICE

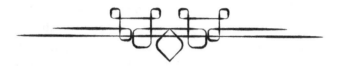

If you've only recently begun studying magic, many of the processes here are going to be difficult for you to undertake successfully, and some might prove downright frustrating. I don't say this to discourage you, but rather to encourage you to take your path at a pace that's wholly right for you. As with any art, getting really good at magic takes time and old-fashioned practice. Don't try to fly before you have wings but also don't hold yourself back. In other words, recognize both your talents and your limitations, and your magical life will unfold far more positively.

More than anything else, be patient with yourself, master the "Witchcraft 101" information, and then return to these methods when you've got a good grasp of the basics. If you're not sure about whether you're ready for adept processes yet, refer to the Leap of Faith in Chapter One. This outlines the foundations necessary to move on to more advanced magical techniques. It also tells you in a step-by-step format what you can do if you haven't wholly built these foundations yet.

By the way, for those of you who may be wondering about what some of the terms in this book mean, a *Priest*

Author's Note to the Novice

or *Priestess* of the Craft is the same as a Priest or Priestess in any religious setting. This person has earned a place of respect through training and study. Sometimes they are an elder, a person of around retirement age, who has been in the Craft for dozens of years. In other cases, it may be a younger individual who has simply grasped the deeper meanings of the Craft and put them to use in a group setting, thereby gaining everyone's respect—and a leadership position.

Similarly, an *adept* or *magus* is someone who has a well-rounded understanding of magical arts, and the ability to put that knowledge to work successfully. These people, and others like them, are some of the best representatives of our community. My hope is that, in time, you can walk a mile in their shoes. I wish you much good fortune and wisdom in this journey.

INTRODUCTION

> *"Magic is 50 percent perspiration, 49 percent inspiration, and 1 percent miracle."*
>
> —The LoreSinger

The modern magical movement, and interest in Witchcraft specifically, began manifesting around the 1970s with an upsurge in ecologically and spiritually minded New Age thinking. During the early years of exploration, ardent seekers read the beginner's "Wicca 101" books, attended magical gatherings, purchased all manner of mystical tools, and learned simple spellcraft. They also performed seasonal rituals, meditated, discussed life's energy matrix with like-minded folks, and began to understand how magic works in both solitary and group settings.

Today, we find that these same seekers have come of age and are ready to take the next step toward personal and spiritual maturity. Knowing exactly what constitutes this next step, however, can be difficult. In a world of seemingly Shake 'n' Bake shamanism and instant Priesthood, the route to *true* magical mastery isn't traversed quickly or without sacrifice, and it can't be found in the yellow pages. So, what does a serious student and seeker—one who wants excellence and quality, not simply a powerful-sounding title like *mage* or *adept*—do?

That's exactly where *Advanced Witchcraft* can help. This book is designed for people who want deeper levels of intuitive awareness and more meaningful, masterful magic. By contacting recognized elders in the magical community for input, I have compiled insights into what it means to be spiritually and magically adept, and some of the metaphysical processes that accompany greater levels of proficiency.

Advanced Witchcraft begins simply by helping you integrate what the Path of Beauty has taught you thus far. The pace of our lives is such that we often accumulate loads of brain knowledge about magical constructs and correspondences, without the heart knowledge that leads to wisdom and adepthood. Since you can't truly know where you're going until you understand where you've been (and why), this internalization is a very important part of magical competence. Without it, Witchcraft becomes a rote metaphysical process instead of a living, transformational spiritual practice.

Advanced Witchcraft discusses the importance of expressing metaphysical lessons and spiritual ideals externally by living in a uniquely magical way. This sounds simple, but it requires a strong personal commitment to making your spiritual path part of every thought, every deed, and every moment. At its pinnacle, adepthood isn't about impressing people; it's a way of living and being. In other words, the focus in this book is not on "talking the talk," but on "walking the walk."

Like any worthwhile endeavor, being magically adept takes time, patience, and practice. Time and patience encourage personal growth and maturity while practice encourages competence. You have to stick with exercises, activities, and studies like those presented here long enough for them to

Introduction

do some good—long enough for the magic within to wake up and make itself an essential part of your existence.

What constitutes "long enough" depends wholly on you. Spirituality is not a "keeping up with the Joneses" proposition. Just because a friend moves on to more advanced magical procedures doesn't mean you have to follow suit, especially if you don't feel ready. Know your strengths, weaknesses, and limitations, and act accordingly. This bit of wisdom, too, is part of being a true adept. Learn to walk before you run.

Additionally, note that the word *advanced* as presented in this book doesn't necessarily mean "more elaborate or complex." Instead, it refers to an improved understanding of the power in, and responsibility for, magical procedures. It also involves developing an augmented ability to concentrate on difficult or long-term goals and progressing along your spiritual path to techniques that require more precision and caution because of the energies involved.

Each chapter in *Advanced Witchcraft* looks at such techniques in as much detail as space allows. Various approaches to methods ranging from glamoury, trance work, and channeling to divination and calling on spirits are covered, along with pragmatic how-tos, and dos and don'ts for each. No matter how magically proficient you may be, the universe has definitive guidelines that exist for your edification and protection. Staying within these guidelines yields the most positive and personally empowering results.

The path to magical adeptness is not without its bumps and potholes, and it won't make all your mundane problems disappear. If anything, a commitment to spiritual enlightenment and magical mastery often brings failure and frustration as teachers. Setbacks, while a bit discouraging, contain worthwhile lessons, like the value of humility, which apply to not only your spiritual path but your everyday living as well.

Additionally, the road to adepthood is one that never really ends. The more we learn, the more we realize how little we really know of the Divine and Creation. As long as you are growing and searching, however, the world of magic will grow with you. Witchcraft, as a spirituality, advocates positive change and can expand our horizons ever outward to reveal some of the universe's greatest mysteries. This, indeed, is a lifelong adventure, and one well worth embarking on. Blessings to you on your personal journey.

NOTE FROM THE AUTHOR

Witchcraft is a very diverse and personalized spiritual practice that cannot be wholly represented by one book. The information, exercises, and approaches here are only one way, among many, to accomplish your goals. Please bear this in mind while you read, recognizing that you will meet people in the magical community who have different ways of approaching the same issues successfully. Find the methods and vision that work best for you and guard these safely in your heart.

CHAPTER ONE

DEFINING THE ADEPT

"Perfection is attained by slow degrees; it requires the hand of time."

—Voltaire

We have reached a critical juncture in the modern magical movement. After several decades of sorting out our faith, we can no longer grant titles like *Priest, Priestess,* and *elder* lightly or out of convenience. Each time someone declares themselves a "master" (or something similar) without understanding or living that title, it's a tremendous disservice to our spirits, our community, and our true adepts or elders who have earned that designation through hard work, service, study, and diligence.

Note that, as seen in the last sentence, I'm using several honored designations (*elder, master, adept*) interchangeably throughout this book. Most recognized elders in our community are people who have lived long lives and grown wise enough to carry the *adept* title. This is a broad generalization but one that I optimistically hope holds true in reality.

Bearing this in mind, the purpose of this chapter is twofold. First, it examines what it means to be magically adept using various archetypes from history and literature. From these examples I've assembled a checklist of sorts that provides a pretty sound profile of *true* adepts and elders. This checklist will help you recognize the important spiritual milestones in your own life: milestones that indicate the maturity necessary for becoming a guide and mentor to others struggling along the path.

Second, this chapter discusses taking the leap of faith necessary to follow the path toward adepthood yourself. Not everyone is ready, willing, prepared for, or capable of moving on to more advanced methods; some people never reach this place in their spiritual development. It is up to you to discern what you're really ready for and how much of yourself you're willing to give to that goal. Don't rush this decision. Meditate, pray, wait, and listen until you feel the spirits calling you, urging you onward.

ARCHETYPES OF ADEPTHOOD

The word *adept* comes from the Latin *adeptus*, meaning "to arrive." The term was originally used by alchemists to describe someone skilled enough to discover either a panacea or the philosopher's stone…no small task, that! Combining this idea with the dictionary guidelines creates a partial image of an adept or elder.

First, adepts are those who "arrive" at a level of proficiency, knowledge, talent, and wisdom that increases their success in the magical arts and inspires respect and admiration from their peers. Second, adepts give something back to their art. Just as a painter's or sculptor's gift is the completed work, adepts' gift is sharing what they've learned, acting as role models, and generally inspiring or challenging people to reach new levels of spiritual awareness. Again, no small task!

In a broad spiritual sense, adepts are not gender specific. While they may externally present as one gender, adepts internally accept and integrate the positive attributes of all genders. This provides them with a delicate balance. The first balancing act stands between diverse energies (such as masculine and feminine or animal and human), allowing adepts to work effectively with more than one theme or range of magical applications at a time.

The second edge balances adepts carefully between the esoteric and mundane. Our spiritual lives cannot be separated from reality if they're to have meaning and transformational power. On the other hand, spiritual pursuits shouldn't take precedence over serious mundane matters. After all, it's hard to respect a teacher who speaks about personal empowerment while his family is being neglected.

There are several literary and historical figures we can look to in helping us further define the role and abilities of adepts. For example, stage magicians like Doug Henning who, before his passing in 2000, illustrated what mystical illusion (such as glamoury; see Chapter Four) can accomplish in skilled hands. Considering this man's chimerical talent, what could Mr. Henning achieve by adding metaphysics to his formula? Even without this dimension, his ability to shift and redirect attention, change appearances, and make things "invisible" is what an adept glamourist would hope to achieve through different methods. In the end, this adept model teaches us to bend energy in a very specific way. After all, "magic is to bend and change."

A second illustration of the adept comes to us from Arthurian legend, namely Merlin. Here, we find the classical magus who speaks with animals, shapeshifts, commands ancient spirits and powers, travels the astral plane without a ticket, knows how to alter the weather, and takes on apprentices to keep the tradition alive. Apply this list of talents to modern Witches and you'll see that several abilities have been lost over time, or perhaps they were shut down due to misuse.

For example, few practitioners today know how to commune with animals other than the occasional telepathic relay between themselves and a familiar. I also don't know many adept weather magicians. It's likely no coincidence that both practices deal with nature, a source of power that has been corrupted and tainted by human hands. So, at least one of the chores of the modern adept is helping undo the damage to Earth's body and spirit using magical and mundane means. Such efforts will begin the process of reclaiming our ancient magical birthrights (like speaking with animals), which in turn continues to stimulate Earth-first, reciprocal living.

The third archetype to consider is that of Taliesin from Welsh lore. After drinking Cerridwen's brew of inspiration, Taliesin was able to confound anyone with riddles and spin powerful magic with songs and words. In true bardic tradition, Taliesin is the bearer of an ancient oral tradition that kept histories and mystical secrets alive, often shrouded in enigmatic, clever phrases.

Through this adept, we see the power of words (especially in spellcasting), the strength of history and tradition (as evidenced in ritual), and the importance of passing along our knowledge in ways that people can understand and remember. We also learn that knowledge is power, some of which can be harmful to those not ready for it. So, rather than giving the proverbial handgun to a child, the adept wisely provides simple, step-by-step instructions and thought-provoking riddles to get us growing at a pace that's right for our heart and spirit.

The final adept model for this chapter is the Magician card in the Tarot. This card is numbered 1, symbolizing singularity of purpose and authority. While artistic renderings differ, the Magician is usually featured with traditional magical tools laid upon their table, ready to be used. In this manner, the adept reminds us to always be prepared, especially to offer our skills when a need arises. They also gently remind us that the most vital tool to our magic is the self; everything else is but symbolic trappings and helpmates.

The Magician's right hand is toward the sky while the left points to Earth, as if embracing all of Creation. This positioning represents the adept's intimate understanding of the ancient maxim, "as above, so below" and the ability to use universal energy to effect changes through willpower. It also represents an awareness that Earth is a sacred space, an altar, upon which we lay out our magic in the hopes of effecting the greatest good.

When the Magician card appears in a Tarot reading, it indicates a calm understanding and self-assurance developing within the questioner, the inner knowingness of the adept. It also symbolizes growing acceptance of psychic gifts as part of the personal transformation process toward mastery. The unseen world begins opening its doors to the magician, if we but dare to look and truly see. When our spiritual eyes do finally open, we will find our magical place, our sense of being, there waiting for us along with a whole new dimension of living: the sphere of the adept.

Historical and literary archetypes show us that adepts or elders:

- Reclaim ancient knowledge, tradition, and powers, keeping them alive for future generations;
- Safeguard magical history so that we can learn from the past in building the future;
- Personally accept the responsibility implied by gaining and using mystical knowledge and skill;

- Honor the Earth as a sacred space and use its resources wisely;
- Acknowledge that life is an act of worship and strive to keep their words and actions in accord;
- Respect individual diversity, knowing there are many paths to enlightenment;
- Embrace creativity and change as fundamental necessities in keeping magic vital;
- Encourage balance in all things;
- Teach others the ways of magic in simple, understandable steps;
- Offer metaphysical aid, consultation, and insights freely to those in need, without personal expectations of gain;
- Give back something to their art or to those who practice it;
- Realize that tools are only helpmates to magic. Real power comes from the mind and heart and will work in harmony with the Earth, spirits, and the Divine;
- Know that mastery is a lifelong process that begins with mastering the self; and…
- Don't have to say who they are. Their lives and actions speak for them.

THE LEAP OF FAITH

If you wish to follow the Path of Beauty and develop your magic further like the adepts and elders of the past, it requires nothing less than integrating the lesson of the Fool card in the Tarot. In this system of cartomancy, the Fool is numbered 0, the number of beginnings and endings, the magic circle, life's cycles, and the undefinable essence of Spirit. Thus, the Fool is not a "foolish" person; it is instead a symbol of the unseasoned, intuitive, spiritual self.

Like you, the Fool stands in an in-between place feeling pushed and pulled by many powers: that which has been, that which is yet to come. The Fool pauses momentarily at the edge of a cliff, representing a vital personal choice. Here, the Fool waits before taking the leap of faith and asks if you are ready and willing to follow. The mundane world is behind, the potential of committed magical living lies ahead. Somewhere between these two, you must jump—away from worldly notions of spirituality, toward challenging the human spirit, and forward to a new beginning.

The Fool's leap of faith can be rather daunting. The cliff seems immense and overwhelming; the bottom is invisible and amorphous, like the future. Suddenly *you* have to trust yourself, the universe, the Divine, and your own inherent magical insights to let your spirit fly instead of fall. But I can assure you that your spirit will take to wing and grow in amazing ways in that glorious moment when you truly believe that *you can.*

We begin practicing Witchcraft with spiritual enlightenment, universal awareness, and reunification with the Sacred Parent as goals, but we also seek self-mastery and a deeper understanding of magical mysteries. Now we stand at a spiritual crossroads, and a decision needs to be made: stay comfortable and work with familiar tried-and-true methods or move forward using these methods as a substructure to advanced practices.

This is not an easy choice, and it's one you should consider carefully. Think of it this way: you would not use a professional power tool without getting training and instructions on how to use it safely and effectively, right? Well, advanced Witchcraft *is* that power tool. It's not a toy or something to try for a trippy spiritual experience. This is serious magic, and the choice to wield it requires sincere, serious thought.

To help with your decision process, look over the list of what adepts do (pages 9-10), and see how many of these attributes have begun manifesting in your life. Also answer the following questions, which indicate some general milestones you should attain before taking the leap of faith, and helpful hints on reaching these milestones if you have not already:

Do you know how to create your own spells, charms, and rituals using sound magical constructs and correspondences?

Advice: Get together with experienced practitioners and discuss what they've found to be successful. Compare these to some of your favorite books and find the methods that feel right and works dependably.

Do you have the capacity to meditate without being easily distracted for more than twenty minutes at a time?

Advice: Meditation is a "practice makes perfect" proposition. Begin by retraining your mind to focus on one thing for short periods of time (two to three minutes); you can then slowly increase these periods until you reach your goal.

Do you know how to use and combine physical movement, sound, sensual input, and visualization to build and direct power and mental focus?

Advice: The more senses you can bring into your magic, the better it will work, and the more meaning it will naturally have. Don't forget to use your feet and hands to direct energy (perhaps mimicking a hug to yourself in a love spell or opening your arms to release a spell).

Do you understand how to pattern, direct, and follow magical energy to your spiritual event horizon and release it toward your goal from this point?

Advice: Think of energy as a strand of yarn in a huge tapestry. Your job is to weave this strand into the pattern so that the fibers don't unravel and so you can create the picture you want. In creating magic, braid this energy strand into your tapestry, taking it as far as you can in your mind and heart, then release the end to Spirit to guide the rest.

Do you understand the symbolism of the circle?

Advice: Think of the circle as a mingling Earth, humankind, the cycles of our lives, and the powers of Creation without time—without beginning or end. Within this protected spiritual sphere, we honor these powers (Earth, Air, Fire, Water) and the Spirit that binds and balances them. This is also a clean, controlled atmosphere within which to build energy for specific goals, then release it toward these goals.

Do you know how to invoke the directional and elemental powers for assistance in things other than ritual work?

Advice: Take time to meditate and commune with each element—perhaps taking a bath for Water, standing in a strong wind for Air, observing a candle for Fire, and running your fingers through soil for Earth. As you do, consider what types of rituals and spells each element could accent, and note these in your journal. A magical journey is like a diary. You keep records of your favorite spells, rituals, prayers, and charms here, alongside your dreams, divination readings, notes from gatherings, and the like. If you're not familiar with creating such a collection, you can get many insights from my book *Your Book of Shadows* (Crossed Crow Books, 2025).

Do you understand the symbolism of the pentagram, and how to use that knowledge in metaphysical procedures (spells, meditations, and the like)?

Advice: Return to the circle within which the pentagram resides and meditate on it in that atmosphere. Like a sacred circle, the pentagram symbolizes all four elements, plus the self, all bound together with Spirit. In the center of all this lies our magic, which ignites when everything works harmoniously together.

Do you know how to find and use creative alternatives for elemental and magical symbols and tools?

Advice: Don't get hung up on using a goblet when a coffee cup, bowl, or seashell might suffice. Or use a wooden spoon, a pencil, or your finger to direct energy. Remember, tools in and of themselves are only symbolic helpmates. You activate the latent potential in them through willpower and concentration.

Do you rely on yourself, willpower, mental focus, and the Divine (or universal energy) for enacting magic, and its successful outcomes, versus tools and props?

Advice: In the end, the only thing you need for magic is *you*. No amount of nifty jewelry, fancy robes, or crystals is a substitute for good old-fashioned self-confidence, faith, and determination.

Do you know and practice magical and psychic self-defense, and know how to wield elemental, visualized, and verbalized banishings when needed?

Advice: This is very important. Do not move on to adept processes until you know how to shield yourself and your home. Similarly, it's vital to understand banishings. You wouldn't leave your house wide open when you go on vacation, right? Well, you don't want to leave it (or you) open to any stray spiritual visitors that may not have your best interest at heart during magical workings. So, return to your basic books, like Marian Weinstein's *Psychic Self Defense,* and learn these techniques.

Do you support your magic with concrete mundane efforts?

Advice: This is also a must. Don't expect the universe, one spell, or one ritual to do all the work for you. For example, after casting a spell for improved finances, begin looking through the want ads, bless your resumes, balance your checkbook, make a new budget, take on more responsibilities at work, and ask for a raise! This gives your magic six good opportunities to start manifesting.

Do you know how to control personal auric energy, how to sense and work with the energy of others, and how to use this awareness in the context of group workings?

Advice: Most people can recognize auric energy in body heat, but it is much more than that. Our thoughts, feelings, and magic all get conveyed through this medium. The first step here is becoming aware of people's personal space. If you notice yourself or someone else becoming uncomfortable, you're awfully close to that intimate auric envelope. This happens a lot in crowded areas like elevators and subways. Try visualizing a white-blue tranquil light filling the air around yourself and see if this doesn't calm everyone down! If so, you've taken a giant leap forward in your ability to work with auras.

Have you developed at least one psychic talent to some degree—divination, past-life reading, object reading, or the like? (Note that you may have done so and not be aware of it.)

Advice: The human mind has amazing potential that we are now only beginning to understand. Never limit your possibilities. Nearly anyone can learn a divination method and use it to begin unlocking the psychic self. Tarot cards and many other divinatory techniques include symbols that are intended to stimulate our spiritual nature. All you need to do is try, practice, and trust your instincts.

One ability in particular that a lot of people overlook is auric reading. This is a kind of psychism that allows you to pick up tensions and moods from people or places. If you can walk into someone's house and immediately know people are fighting, some of your psychic talents are already waking up. Likewise, if you always know when friends need you, that's a kind of telepathy or empathy. Now you just need to hone these abilities so you can tap in whenever you wish.

Do you find the basic Witchcraft books leaving you wanting? Do they seem too rudimentary or superficial—as if a dimension is missing as you read?

Advice: Read more! There's no such thing as too much knowledge unless it's unused or unapplied. Take the best advice that you find in several unrelated texts, blend together things that augment your path, then move on.

If you can answer yes to most of these, you probably have a strong-enough background in Witchcraft and the magical basics to consider advanced magical approaches. Again, this is only a general guide. You must determine in your mind, heart, and spirit if the time is truly right for you.

MAKING A COMMITMENT

If, after considering the aforementioned points, you decide that you have the training, knowledge, and attitude necessary for following the Adept's Path, then you've figuratively jumped off the Fool's cliff and started to soar. But now the question is, where do you fly? Where exactly is this adventure leading? The answer to this question is different for each individual. One thing that will help you find a partial answer is putting your commitment into the context of a ritual. Rituals give our magical energy and goals a functional construct and shape, akin to the way a glass shapes water.

Basically, a ritual like the one given here expresses your aim to the universe, gods, and spirits. It is not something to enter into lightly. You will be making a promise to the Sacred Powers to follow through, to walk the path no matter how long or how difficult and to accept the personal changes and responsibilities this will bring.

If you go ahead with the ritual, I suggest reading it through from beginning to end. Make any personally meaningful changes in the wording, components, movements, and so forth. Remember: this ritual is between you, the Ancients, and your Divine. Only your heart and soul can tell you how it should be done so that it really empowers and inspires your goal. This particular ritual is written for a solitary practitioner, but it can easily be adapted for group use, if desired.

DEDICATION RITUAL

The Altar: Place your personal magical tools (an athame or ritual knife, a brazier, a cup or cauldron, and the like) on the altar in a way that is pleasing to you and reflects your own personal tradition. In the center of the altar, have a triangle of lit candles (one yellow, one silver, and one green) around an unlit white candle. These three represent body, mind, and spirit, centered on the Divine. Also have ready an anointing oil whose aroma and ingredients, to you, represent commitment, inner peace, awareness, and wisdom (a blend of sandalwood, sage, rose, and lavender is one good choice).

The Circle: Create the sacred space using personally significant elemental markers. Consider having elementally colored candles at the four points ready to be lit as you invoke the quarters. Alternatively, have something suited to the element that you can pour out or sprinkle to denote this power's presence in the sacred space: seeds or grain for Earth, potpourri or feathers for Air, a libation of water or wine for Water, and a candle for Fire.

Also, set up the circle so that the entryway and the exit are across from one another. This way, you can go out opposite from where you entered (symbolically denoting a change in your path's focus).

Clothing: Purely personal. Some people prefer to enact this skyclad so that the trappings of the mundane world do not stand between them and the Divine. Others like to wear one robe into the circle and don another after the final spoken words to mark their personal transition.

Incense: Keep this simple, like myrrh, sandalwood, or frankincense to emphasize spirituality. Gently move this around the sacred space before beginning, using a prayer feather (this symbolizes your desire for gentle, yet potent, speech and actions suited to the duties of an adept).

Invocation: This begins in the East to mark a new beginning and hope, then moves clockwise around the circle.

> *East: "Powers of the East, awake in me. (Light the candle.) Bring the winds of change to this sacred space and my questing spirit. Let your protective breezes guide and steer me, as they wrap around this circle, bearing witness to my heart's promise."*
>
> *South: "Powers of the South, burn in me. (Light the candle.) Bring the embers of magic to this sacred space and my questing spirit. Let your protective fires guide and clarify my path as they surround this circle, bearing witness to my heart's promise."*
>
> *West: "Powers of the West, flow through me. (Light the candle.) Bring the waters of inspiration to this sacred space and my questing spirit. Let your protective waves motivate me as they surround this circle, bearing witness to my heart's promise."*
>
> *North: "Powers of the North, root in me. (Light the candle.) Bring the soil of growth to this sacred space and my questing spirit. Let your protective earth guide*

and nurture me as it surrounds this circle, bearing witness to my heart's promise."

Center: "Ancient Ones, Goddess and God, join me in this place beyond all space and time. Witness this rite, and the promise I make. Keep me true to myself, my path, and you as I embark on this journey. So mote it be."

Turn toward the altar, taking in hand the green candle and saying:

"I give my body to serve the greatest good. May it remain a strong and healthy temple as I begin my journey toward magical mastery."

Light the white candle with this flame, then replace the candle on the altar. Take the yellow candle in hand, saying:

"I give my mind to serve the greatest good. May it remain focused and keen as I begin my journey toward adepthood."

Add the fire from this flame to that of Spirit, then replace the candle on the altar. Take the silver candle in hand, saying:

"I give my spirit to serve the greatest good. May it remain pure and loving as I begin my journey toward spiritual enlightenment."

Add the fire from this flame to that of Spirit, then replace the candle on the altar.

Next, dab a bit of anointing oil on the palms of your hands and hold them facedown over your magical tools.

Visualize a white-gold light pouring into them, then invoke the blessings of your personal spirits or deities in using the tools with words like:

"(Spirits/Deity), these tools have served me well on the Path of Beauty. Bless and purify them so my magic flows through each in perfect love and perfect trust. As I embark on this great quest, help me to slowly free myself from needing or depending on such things, using them only as helpmates. Help me to know, in my heart and spirit, that the magic is me—that I enable mystical energy through my will and focused resolve. So mote it be."

Afterward, take the anointing oil again and begin a rite of self-blessing:

At the crown chakra: "Bless me that I may always remain open to the guidance of Spirit."

At the temples: "Bless my mind that it may focus and direct my magic with the powers of reason and intuition."

At the Third Eye: "Bless my vision that I may remain open to the psychic, spiritual self and its insights."

At the mouth: "Bless my words that I might speak with wisdom and act accordingly."

At the heart: "Bless my heart that it might freely give and receive love, including self-love."

At the hands: "Bless my hands for service."

At the feet: "*Bless my feet that they may never stray from the path before me and walk sure in my magical tradition.*"

At this point, I strongly advocate a time of meditation and introspection. Consider all the reasons why you've taken this step, and what you hope to achieve by so doing. Place your dreams and visions of your spiritual future before the Divine, praying for counsel and assistance in any way that feels right. Don't hurry this time. Let the seriousness of the moment really sink in, and the power of your rite fill you. If you have a magical journal, this would be a good time to write your impressions of this juncture, and to list some specific goals for the coming year. Then, close the circle starting in the North to indicate your desire for strong foundations and personal maturity:

North: "*Farewell, Earth Spirits that shape and hold the soils of the Mother. Thank you for being here to cultivate strong roots beneath my goal. Feed and water them, and my growing spirit within and without this sacred space.*"

West: "*Farewell, Water Spirits that wash and flow with healing and emotion. Thank you for being here to cleanse my spirit. Fill always the well of my soul with your essence within and without this sacred space.*"

South: "*Farewell, Fire Spirits, that spark and dance with power and energy. Thank you for being here to ignite my soul anew. Keep the flames of truth and light burning in my heart within and without this sacred space.*"

> East: *"Farewell, Air Spirits, that gust and sing with hope and inspiration. Thank you for being here to motivate and guide my transformation. Keep the winds of fresh beginnings always at my back within and without this sacred space."*

> Center: *(This should be a personal prayer, directed to your vision of the Divine. Here is a sample.)* *"I call upon the Mighty Ones to stand before me to guide my path. Help me to walk it gently and with an understanding of the responsibility that goes with power. Help me study diligently, seeking after the deeper mysteries. Help me integrate what I learn and apply it daily in my life that I might become the magic in word and deed. So be it."*

After the ritual, ground yourself with simple foods like fresh vegetables. Crunchy foods bring your energy back to normal and will help you begin your path to adepthood with both feet on the ground.

You may want to consider reenacting this ritual once a year on its anniversary date as a way of recommitting your spirit to the task ahead. Reread your journal entries from the previous year to see how your spirit has grown. Make another list of goals for the coming year, then ask the Divine to help you manifest those aims in your closing prayer.

LIVING THE MAGIC

Adeptness is a lifetime proposition. No one becomes a magical authority overnight, or by performing one ritual. The universe is a very big place with nooks and crannies of spiritual insight hidden everywhere. For as long as you live, there will always be another "brass ring" to reach for along the path to mastery. This keeps us from becoming complacent or egotistical by offering ongoing spiritual challenges that motivate, inspire, empower, and sometimes confound us.

So, how exactly do we find these brass rings? Some of the best advice here comes from the wisdom of Buddha, who felt that uncovering any spiritual truth really boils down to staying awake! We need to wake up from our mundane slumber long enough to see possibilities and potentials—long enough to integrate new magic approaches and methods into our everyday existence.

We need to stay awake to see the changes in ourselves, others, Earth, and the universe so our magical path grows and changes alongside that transformation. We need to stay awake so our path doesn't become stagnant, which kills the magic. We need to stay awake, tending the fires of Spirit so they don't fade, taking the Light that guides our path with them.

In other words, the path of the adept, the way to practicing advanced Witchcraft, includes a wake-up call. No more "fluffy bunny white light energy." No more excuses for neglected spiritual hygiene. No more wishy-washy, watered-down magic. This is a path of power and until we truly believe this, our faith will remain as milk-toast instead of meat.

When you finally discover this inner assurance, it will motivate you onward, and reaching important spiritual objectives will follow quite naturally. As they do, give each landmark along your path some special attention. Take time out to recognize the milestone, pat yourself on the back, and integrate the associated lessons. Think of this process as akin to jumping hurdles. If you rush forward in the magical progression too quickly, without using sound judgment and learning from the past, you're likely to fall flat. Instead, stop and assess what you've learned and how it changes your vision of magic. Then, move on using this knowledge as a key to finding, reaching, and overcoming the next challenge.

Also, use the knowledge gained at each juncture to express magical principles externally. Remember, action follows magic, and manifestation follows action. Each time your life depicts your magical path (and changes in it)—each time living *becomes* the magic—you naturally facilitate all previously cast spells or rituals. Herein is the real power and potential of the adept. It is not all bundled into, or hinged upon, one metaphysical process but manifests in every moment of every day in thought, word, and deed.

WHAT TO EXPECT ALONG THE WAY

Practicing Witchcraft changes your life in interesting and unexpected ways. And while these changes differ from person to person, the path of the adept seems to generate some shifts almost universally. Using the old adage "forewarned is forearmed," this section reviews a few of these shifts, and how to handle them when they come.

First, even individuals who have a solitary practice will discover other people seeking them out, looking for answers or hope. This is a natural effect of honest magical living, so be prepared, but don't revel in the notoriety. Remember, you're human, with human failings that people will be happy to point out when you mess up. You cannot fix every problem, mend every argument, and organize every event, or you *will* burn out.

Also, it's not always your job to jump in with aid; the universe might be trying to teach someone self-sufficiency! Practicing advanced Witchcraft means, in part, learning how and when to say no. Then, as the universe calls upon your talents, you have the energy and wherewithal to respond.

Second, people may begin asking you to lead a study group or coven, put together a newsletter, speak at public gatherings, and the like. As they do, remember that not every person making a serious effort to become adept is called to lead, to publish, to speak, or whatever. In fact, most have very specific talents that the universe augments and uses instead of trying to put a proverbial square peg in a round hole.

For example, someone with musical talent may begin playing at gatherings or even recording an album, but they won't necessarily lecture. Someone with writing skills might put together a newsletter or book but they won't necessarily lead a group. While some type of community service is part of an adept's responsibility, the forms this service takes can be as diverse as humanity itself. Don't let enthusiastic, good-intentioned folks pressure you into awkward or inappropriate roles. The only person who can determine what external representations of your path are right for you is *you*. (See also Chapter Eight, "Serving the Community.")

Third, nearly everyone I spoke to said that when they took the step toward practicing advanced Witchcraft, a lot of stupid shit started happening to them. Cars broke down, mail got lost, wallets got stolen, and a huge laundry list of other ensuing frustrations occurred. I see two possible reasons for this.

For one, there are negative energy forces in the universe that would prefer that good Witches didn't gain more proficiency. These negative thought-forms might use inconvenience as a distraction to keep your mind on things other than your studies. If you believe this is the case, then start cleansing the sacred space of your home and reinforcing your magical and psychic wards regularly to combat the problem.

Alternatively, these problems and obstacles may act as teachers of a sort. If we allow circumstances to distract us from the goal of magical proficiency, then we're likely not ready for the responsibility that goes with it. Even when life gets hectic, magic should be part of our thoughts and actions in some way. Focus is a key to adepthood, as are awareness and insight. In other words, don't sweat the small stuff, and keep a good sense of humor as an ally in your quest. This will often serve you better than any number of books.

Fourth, your impressions of self, the Craft, others, and the world are going to transform. The road toward mastery develops self-confidence, magical artistry, thoughtfulness, and gentle reciprocity with nature. These developments mirror what's happening in your spirit and reveal the personal progress of which you should be very proud.

So, what should you expect? My advice is to be prepared for anything and everything. Stay open to the universe and its leadings, remain focused on your goal, and keep reading, sharing, and caring. This is a marvelous, exciting juncture in your spiritual life. Your magical and spiritual future is now an open book, just waiting for you to turn the page!

CHAPTER TWO

A MOMENT'S PAUSE

"The true order of learning should be: first, what is necessary; second, what is useful; and third, what is ornamental. To reverse this arrangement is like beginning to build at the top of the edifice."

—George Fillmore Swain

By the definition given in Chapter One, an adept is someone who arrives at a different mental and spiritual space, one with a different way of approaching magic with more erudition, discernment, and prudence. Be that as it may, it's difficult to arrive from this place without first departing from someplace else. Consequently, this chapter temporarily departs from exploring more advanced processes. I'll ask you to pause for a moment—just long enough to truly recognize and integrate what you've learned in magic thus far and what it means to you in body, mind, and spirit.

I know you're likely anxious to move forward, but each level of spiritual attainment requires a momentary sojourn for integration to occur. Let's face it, life moves very quickly these days, leaving little time to digest all the changes this brings to our spirits. And since Witches have no particular Bible to follow, it's even more difficult to gauge spiritual progress. To make matters worse, every person's vision of Witchcraft and magic can be slightly different, with similarly diverse growing paces. In other words, there's no norm against which we can calibrate our personal magical advancements, other than ourselves!

Despite these unique quandaries, you really know a lot more about magic than you might realize on an intuitive level, if not consciously. For example, you can probably explain the basics of spellcasting and how to use willpower to direct that energy without much thought. You can also likely recite the uses of traditional magical tools and the significance of the Wheel of the Year in your sleep.

But how has this knowledge affected you? Has it altered the way you live? It should, and it probably has. Many people don't notice these changes, however, because of life's chaos and mundane responsibilities! The purpose of the next section is to help you overcome this problem.

RECOGNITION

If you're like most serious magical seekers I've met, you hold faith as important enough that it's already showing signs of leaking into your everyday life. This is a good indication of spiritual development and one that you should pay attention to whenever it occurs, now or in the future. The exercises here are designed to open your eyes and keep you awake to all the wonderful transformations magic and Witchcraft can bring to your life and outlook every day.

Application One: Connections

Get a piece of paper and a pen, and take a deep, centering breath. Close your eyes and relax for a few minutes. Think back over the months or years of your involvement in the Craft. As you remember personally significant events, write down all the ways in which you feel magic has changed your life at home, at work, in bed, in relationships, or whatever. As you describe one area, think of other interrelated situations that may be affected peripherally. For example, if your kids' attitudes have been changed by the Craft, what about their playmates or their playmates' parents? It's all connected!

To stress these connections, try patterning your answers in this exercise on paper to form a tree or web. In my life, for example, I see Witchcraft strongly affecting my relationships, which then affects my self-confidence, my effectiveness in my work, the way others perceive me, and so on.

For those who find free flow writing difficult, try painting, drawing, using a voice recorder, or typing out your ideas. I promise you'll find the results interesting, if not enlightening. Magic travels along branching sequences that grow geometrically. Consequently, it has far-reaching effects that we often don't recognize until thoughtful moments of introspection and expression. This activity and the formulation of this chart show you firsthand how many people, places, and things have been affected by your beliefs and efforts. It's an eye-opening and empowering experience.

Application Two: Mirror, Mirror

For this application, you need little other than a mirror, your magical journal, and some privacy. In this case, I want you to focus wholly on things about yourself that have changed since you first decided to practice Wicca. Think back to those first few weeks, months, or the entire first year—how excited you were, how naive and, in many cases, overwhelmed and thrilled by finally finding a belief system that fit you just right.

Now look in the mirror. If it helps you to concentrate, you can light a candle nearby to create a magical ambience. Trace an invoking pentagram with your finger thrice on the surface of the mirror, saying each time you trace the symbol:

> *"Mirror, mirror show to me,*
> *grant me eyes with which to see;*
> *Reveal to me my spirit's path,*
> *who I've been and who I'll be."*

Let your words lead you into a deeper level of meditation and spiritual openness. Slowly let your vision blur as you continue watching the surface of the mirror for images to appear. These may be literal or symbolic in nature.

Write down whatever you see, then come back to it later to ponder its significance. For example, if you see two halves of a heart slowly knitting together, it might mean that an emotional healing is occurring in your life thanks to focused magical efforts. For more ideas on how to interpret these images, look to a dream interpretation guide like *Language of Dreams,* a divination encyclopedia like *Futuretelling,* or a symbolic dictionary like *The Illustrated Book of Signs & Symbols* (see the bibliography).

Afterward, take another deep breath and relax for a few minutes. Read over the first entry you ever made in your magical journal, then read the second-to-last. Or think about the first ritual or spell you ever helped with, and then the last one. Compare the two. How have your impressions of your magical self, spiritual ideals and metaphysical processes, or ways of working magic transformed over time? How are these changes significant to who you are and how you live today? Make a list of the changes and read it periodically to reinforce the learning process. You can also read it as a pick-me-up whenever you get discouraged.

Now look forward in time a bit. Make a list of goals for the coming weeks, months, and years. What spiritual changes do you want to see by this time next year? What topics or traditions would you like to study? What attributes do you wish to develop, and what magical insights do you want to improve? Keep this list in a safe place. Anytime you reenact this application, or other similar introspective exercises, review the list and see how many goals you've achieved. This way you can gauge your growth in definable, personally meaningful terms.

Application Three: What's in a Name

Many Witches choose to use a special name when performing ritual or working magic. This is a name they've chosen for themselves, one that somehow reflects the best of who they are and all they hope to be. For the purposes of this exercise, I want you to get a good name and write your chosen magical name on a large piece of paper.

Think back to when you chose this name. What was it that drew you to the vibrations of this designation? Write down various words that come to mind in connection with your name around it.

Next, look up the meaning of your magical name in the dictionary. Does the meaning there mirror what you hoped to illustrate, the principles and goals you wished reflected in it? What aspirations did you have for your magical path at that time, and which have since been reached?

Now say your name three times out loud. Feel the energy in it. Sense the vibrations. Is this energy something that will continue to inspire your maturation as a magical being—or have you outgrown the name? Many people seriously seeking the Adept's Path will find that the first magical name they chose is, indeed, outmoded and somewhat immature. Now is the time to choose anew!

In many religious traditions, a drastic change in path is accompanied by a reflective name change, and the Adept's Path is no different. Take your time and look through that name dictionary again. Look through books on the ancient gods, goddesses, heroines, and heroes. Consider great literary figures for their positive attributes. Choose a serious name (Merlin is *not* a good choice) that somehow reveals who you are now and who you hope to become in the process of spiritual transformation.

Please realize that since the path to adepthood doesn't end until you do, you may find you outgrow this designation, too. When you do, rejoice in that maturity, find your new name, and move on.

Application Four: Outlooks

After digesting the ways in which Witchcraft has defined and changed your perceptions of the self, the next step is seeing how it has altered your perceptions of others, the world, the universe, and the Divine. For the purposes of this activity, I suggest thinking back to your outlooks in the year prior to practicing the Craft.

As before, take a few deep, cleansing breaths and really center yourself. Let all other thoughts recede; focus on the task at hand. First, concentrate on your perceptions of other people. Ask yourself questions like: did you carry certain prejudices that have faded? Are you more appreciative of the sacredness of others now? Can you sense people's energy without trying, whereas before it was a "best guess" proposition? Are you more tolerant of other people's beliefs now than you were a year ago?

Next, think about your outlooks regarding the earth. Have you begun recycling or picking up litter when before it might have gone by the wayside? Do you ride a bike or take the bus sometimes to decrease harmful emissions into the ecosystem? Are you more sensitive to nature's cycles and how they affect you? Do you often intuitively know when the weather is changing without the help of the six o'clock news? Do you feel a stronger kinship with animals now than you did before? Can you sometimes empathically understand their messages? And what about plants and stones? How have your perspectives about these natural objects changed? Can you sense their energy matrix?

The third step is a little more difficult. It might help to perform this part of the exercise outdoors at night. Look up to the stars and the expanse of space. What did this view mean to you prior to practicing magic? Do you have a different idea of what makes up the universe now than you did before? Consider: the human spirit and potential are as vast and sweeping as this wonder! That potential includes *you*.

Finally, how do you perceive the Divine (or universal energy)? Was this power an intimate part of your life before practicing the Craft? Have you adopted a patron deity? Do you sense universal or divine energy coursing through people? Places? Things? Yourself? Describe this power and feeling.

When you're done with making these observations, allow yourself several hours over the next few days to reread them. It's going to take a while to assimilate it all. As in the previous activity, I also suggest reading this information over on a regular basis. Each time you do, you're likely to find something you didn't see before, or see it a different way.

Just like children, spiritual seekers go through growth spurts and lulls. I heartily recommend repeating these exercises, or other similar ones, at least once a year. This way, recognizing and appreciating Wiccan ideals, energy, and associated changes becomes part of the rhythm of the years. It also becomes an intimate part of your life's ritual, which is an important step along the Adept's Path.

INTEGRATION AND EXPRESSION

"The great art of learning is to undertake but little at a time."
—John Locke

We all carry a heavy load on one serving platter these days. As a result, time for thoughtful introspection is a rare commodity. This means that a great deal of our learning takes place on a cursory level. Every hour of every day, our minds gather a tremendous amount of information and store it. But until we take the time to unlock this storehouse and sift through the materials, it remains head knowledge instead of something we feel, something we express naturally, something we *live*.

We have to make time for internalization to occur. One way is by setting aside a little time daily, or a few hours a week, to devote wholly to the Craft. The amount of time doesn't have to be excessive but do stop your mundane duties long enough to give magic a special place to express itself in your everyday life.

What types of things can you do to integrate and express your spirituality? A lot. Many are easy and not overly time-consuming! Get creative, use your imagination, and look at every moment of living as an opportunity to express your magic. At first, you might have to really think about it, reminding yourself to see even the most mundane activity as something with magical potential. With time and tenacity, however, it becomes natural. This expression of faith will begin walking hand in hand with who you are and everything you do. Here are some fun, functional, and fulfilling ways to get started, or augment what you're already doing:

- Keep some beneficial aromatic herbs or oils in the bathtub so they filter into your aura during baths and showers (like rose to manifest self-love, ginger for energy, or sage for wisdom). Don't forget to chant and sing for a "shower" of blessings or visualize your tensions or sicknesses going down the drain!
- Leave empowered incantations or charged magical items in places around the house where their energy will do the most good. Thinking about the spell each time you pass one will augment its energy. For example, place written communication spells near where you charge your phone at night. Leave a magical sigil for weight loss on the refrigerator, herbs for fertility in your pillow or under the bed, aromatics for harmony in the family room, or peaceful oils on lightbulbs.
- Cook with magically empowered herbs and blessed foods so you can internalize power. For instance, drink tea in the morning for courage before asking for a raise. Make it apple tea if you're feeling under the weather! And don't forget mealtime prayers so that the temple of your soul (the body) is nourished and blessed.
- Start the morning off right with the Divine as a helpmate. Light a candle and say a brief good morning to the universe each day.
- Stick a meaningful symbol of a personal need to your refrigerator with a magnet at breakfast time so it can begin "attracting" that energy into your entire day.

- Augment specific magical energy necessary for coping with your routine by choosing each day's clothing and aromatics according to their metaphysical associations. For example, wear red for power and energy or yellow to improve your communication skills for a meeting. Dab on lilac oil for inner peace and vanilla to accent vitality. Dust your shoes with powdered marjoram so happiness walks with you, or nutmeg for extra luck.
- Pack some of the leftovers from your mystical meals for lunch to keep both you and your magic moving. If possible, get outside with nature during your lunch break to reconnect with the earth. Even in the concrete jungle, you can usually find a sunny bench!
- Speaking of movement, trace positive protective symbols on your car's tires with patchouli oil. Each time the tire turns, it generates energy to keep you safe wherever you go.
- Wherever you go during the day, smile at people. It boosts good karma, generates positive energy, tends to improve your own outlook, and motivates the very special magic of kindness. It also makes people wonder why you're so happy and may even brighten their day!
- When you get home, stop outside the door and flick off any negativity and tension from your day like so much excess water. Visualize your aura being filled with sparkling magical light, then go inside. In this way, the sacred space of your home doesn't get cluttered with bad vibes.
- When cleaning up your living space, play uplifting magical music, burn empowering incense, sing, move clockwise to draw positive energy—anything you can think of to metaphysically stir up harmony in your home.

- At night, light a candle again and say thank you for another day of living and learning. A heart filled with gratitude is also one ready to receive greater lessons and responsibilities.
- Before going to bed, make peace with yourself and others in your home. Magic does not flow freely in a body or home where discord exists. Don't forget to say a prayer for world peace, too—after all, Earth is our mother and teacher.
- As you're going to sleep, meditate and visualize. Focus this time on pressing needs, areas where you need improved perspective, or as a way of invoking insightful dreams. To emphasize the latter, place some balsam needles, roses, and marigold petals beneath your pillow.
- Keep a dream journal or tape recorder near your bed so that if you do receive any inspired, insightful dreams, you can write them down and read them later for edification.

Application Five: Reassessing Daily Focal Points

The previous examples illustrate ways that you can change the focus of everyday activities to something more magical and suited to your path. For this fifth exercise, I want you to reassess your daily routine. Make a list of everything you do on a normal day, from waking to sleeping. Keep it as detailed as possible; don't forget things like brushing your teeth and tying shoes.

Afterward, next to each item on your list, write down as many ways as you can think of to change the *ordinary* into something *extraordinary* by adding a personally meaningful magical method to the equation. For example, you might use knot magic when tying a sneaker or necktie to bind energy into this piece of clothing. Or you could brush your teeth with mint-flavored toothpaste before asking for a raise (mint emphasizes prosperity and protection). Really, the options are as vast as your imagination will allow.

The nice part about this activity is that afterward, you'll find you appreciate the potential magic that everyday life offers much more. You'll also begin noticing more opportunities to sprinkle in a little magic as they occur.

Application Six: Making Time for Magic

I'm sure a lot of you have schedules that—like mine—seem to leave little time for spiritual endeavors. The purpose of this activity is to find time in your schedule that you could use magically with a little inventiveness.

Look over the activity list you compiled for application five. Are there any activities that you could drop periodically to give you more time to study and practice magic? Maybe you could give up the eleven o'clock news twice a week and read or meditate instead. Or you might forgo reading the daily paper once in a while to work on a spell, a special brew, or a uniquely magical meal for your family. Next, review the list again and see if there's void time that could be used for magical purposes. For example, I like to think of pressing questions while I drive, then watch for street signs, bumper stickers, billboards, and license plates that answer my queries. It's a unique type of divination, but it works! How many more hours in the day can you fill similarly just by looking at them differently? I'm willing to bet it will be quite a significant amount.

Application Seven: The Idea Funnel

Another way to integrate spiritual principles is through visualization. Get comfortable, close your eyes, and breathe deeply until you feel yourself reaching a meditative state. Release all the tensions in your body and psychically turn off outside interferences that may disrupt your quiet time.

When you feel ready, see yourself in your mind's eye as you are right now. Above your head envision a silver and gold funnel filled with rainbow-colored lights. As you watch, the lights move and shift as if dancing with joy. They form pictures or phrases that express the various spiritual ideas, knowledge, and attributes you wish to integrate (it sometimes helps to make a list of these ahead of time).

One at a time, as the words, symbols, or phrases form, let them pour down through the funnel into the top of your head, then flow naturally into your heart. Note the difference in how you feel after each word or symbol has rooted in your heart. I find this has a very settling, centering effect. Continue this way until the funnel is empty and you're wholly saturated with light energy. Use this energy in the days ahead to help you outwardly express what's in your heart.

Note: some people find it helpful to record visualizations ahead of time, leaving pauses in appropriate spots so the images can form properly while they listen.

All these things may seem simple but they're very important in the long haul. Adeptness is about living the magic, about becoming wholly united with that sacred energy. Regular maintenance like the exercises here integrates the immenseness of magic, its deeper meanings, and your personal power. It also gives you effective ways to express the significance of the Craft through your daily routine. With time and diligence, this leads to thinking, speaking, feeling, and acting effortless with magic.

MOTIVATION

Once you've recognized and internalized your magical beliefs, experiences, and their associated effects (which, by the way, is an ongoing cycle), it's time to ponder your motivation for starting advanced practices. Among the uninitiated or inexperienced, there is often the mistaken impression that advancement equates to more power, more status, and more authority. If you've been misled similarly, this section will set things straight.

It's natural to hope that advanced practice improves the success of magic and that our leaders are people who have moved on to such levels. Nonetheless, one thing does not naturally follow another, nor should it become the motivation for following the Adept's Path. This is not the time for fudging the rules, ego trips, power plays, exploiting group dynamics, or manipulation. Unfortunately, some people squander magical knowledge and training for just such purposes. These individuals, no matter what they claim, are *not* elders or adepts, because they don't conduct themselves in a manner suited to a positive spiritual role model.

If we're to preserve the honor and integrity of the Craft, it is extremely important that we avoid these tempting pitfalls before entering the Adept's Path, and all the while we walk it. Here are some ideas that will help you maintain a balanced, modest outlook as you go along:

- Listen closely to your conversations. Are you using a lot of jargon and Witchy-sounding words? If so, get down off the soapbox and talk to people in ways they can understand easily. The Craft has been misinterpreted enough without faddish terminology confusing the public even more. Unless you know that someone has some foundational knowledge about magical practices, stick to the KISS (keep it simple) school of explanations.

- Also, listen closely to the way you speak to people new to the Craft, or those outside of it. Don't talk down to them, act bemused by simplistic questions, or cop other similarly highfalutin' attitudes. It's one thing to have confidence and knowledge, and another altogether to cram it down people's throats. "Do unto others" is an excellent motto to follow, no matter what level of mastery you've attained.
- Watch how frequently you flaunt your associations, titles, degrees, and the like. If you find yourself continually talking about being a "_____degree High Priestess" or the like, it's time to reassess yourself and your motives. Remember, the higher you elevate yourself into that ivory tower, the farther you have to fall!
- Allow yourself to be both a teacher and student in spiritual conversations. Just because people are new to magic, or haven't been practicing as long as you, doesn't mean they're without refreshing ideas and perspectives that may help you. Like life, sometimes our magic can get stale. Folks newer to magical traditions rejuvenate our excitement and often give us some real food for thought. As the old saying goes: "Out of the mouths of babes…!"
- Even after you've chosen a tradition, continue to research others for good ideas, novel approaches, and unique insights. Don't get snared in the "my way or the highway" mind-set. There is no one "right" way to practice Witchcraft; all have value, and all can potentially inspire some new methods and thought processes.

- Once a week, set aside a few moments to meditate about what's gone on around you. Did you react to others and situations in a manner suited to the adept or elder? If not, what caught you unawares? Work on these areas of your life over the ensuing days, weeks, and months. No matter how advanced you become, practice still makes perfect.
- Avoid getting entangled in gossip mongering and Witch wars. These do nothing to further the Craft, your respectability as an elder, or your spirituality. They're also a very unproductive use of energy. On the other hand, *do* offer calm, constructive advice to help stop such situations and resolve them positively.
- If you offer a study group, readings, or other magical services for which you charge a fee, make sure that fee is reasonable and doesn't penalize people for having empty pockets. Charging high prices doesn't prove your value or your adeptness. Yes, your time is worth something, and folks do seem to value what they have paid for more highly. Nonetheless, offer sliding-scale fees, and keep your take-home pay out of the "oh my god" range. Money never has, and never will, pave the road to mastery. You can't buy it; it's something you earn. (See also Chapter Eight.)
- Find a few magically minded friends who are willing to become cooperative overseers. You watch them, and they watch you, for signs of inappropriate motivations seeping into spiritual pursuits. When this occurs, you let each other know, using friendship as the binding tie to soothe and correct the difficulties.

- Last but certainly not least, always remember to say "thank you" when your magic manifests. Childlike wonder helps you appreciate the miracle of magic, and a heart full of gratitude is one that rarely misuses its gifts.

ADVANCED WITCHCRAFT: THE HUMAN FACTOR

We're all human and we all have imperfections. In the process of becoming an adept or elder, I can guarantee you will fall flat on your face from time to time (says the author who has multiple bruises on her nose). This is perfectly normal. It's just like a child learning to walk. Take life and magic one step at a time.

So, read on. Try the different techniques given in these pages and see where your spiritual path takes you. When failures come, try not to be too hard on yourself. Just dust yourself off. As long as you learn something from an experience, you can still turn a negative into a positive and keep going. When successes come, rejoice in them, pat yourself on the back, then return to recognizing, internalizing, manifesting, and growing!

CHAPTER THREE
DYNAMIC TRADITIONAL MAGIC

"What an enormous magnifier is tradition! How a thing grows in the human memory and in the human imagination when love, worship, and all that lies in the human heart is there to encourage it."
—Thomas Carlyle

Traditional magic, for the purposes of this book, constitutes spellcasting, charm and amulet creation, ritual weaving, and working with familiars. These methods gained traditional status in two ways. First, they are very popular in the magical community. Second, they are the ones most readily associated with Witchcraft in the public mind.

Elevating traditional magic to a more adept level isn't too difficult. Some of the proficiency necessary already exists just from frequency of use and familiarity. The remainder can be generated by technique-specific additions (discussed below) and by adding the elements of timing and repetition to the equation.

The workday world makes the following of stringent timing edicts for traditional magic difficult. Nonetheless, in looking at common historical examples, it's obvious that the ancient magi relied heavily on empowering astrological signs, lunar phases, Sun signs, and the hour of the day in timing their craft. I will be the first to admit that getting up at two in the morning on a weeknight just to pick an herb is not on my list of fun things to do. Yet I cannot help but believe that our forebears left this information behind for a good reason.

Following the maxim "as above, so below," the ancients believed that all things in the heavens mirror those on Earth and vice versa. As the stars' patterns and the Moon's phases change, they have the capacity to influence life. A good example of this concept was the theory that crazy behavior (that of a *luna*-tic) is governed by the Moon. These types of beliefs created the foundations for using symbolic timing in magic.

Now that we know that stars are only balls of gas and we can now predict exactly when and why the Moon phases occur, do the potentials in using special timing to amplify our magic change as well? I don't think so. In any magical procedure, proper timing from start to finish builds a strong sympathetic foundation, including in the ways you're thinking and acting.

Consider a love spell that calls for basil as a component. What if you were to plant the basil during a waxing to full moon and chant over it every waxing to full moon until harvesting (for growing love), harvest it when the Moon is in Scorpio (for passion), and cast the spell at 2:00 p.m. (an hour that emphasizes partnership and relationships)? All of this would create an amazing thematic matrix for your magical power to follow (like an electrical line, if you will) in manifesting itself. Note that every step in the rather mundane process of gardening here has been transformed by a little metaphysical forethought into a magical procedure or action.

If you're not overly familiar with hourly correspondences and astrological associations, I suggest buying a good astrological calendar. Look to this, and several of your introductory spellcraft and ritual books (like *Spinning Spells, Weaving Wonders* or *A Witch's Book of Ceremonies and Rituals*, both available from Crossed Crow Books) for help. Compare the associations given. Then, decide what dimensions of timing you can add without throwing your entire routine into disarray. For example, if hourly or lunar timing isn't going to be possible because of your work schedule, consider weekday, monthly, or seasonal timing instead.

Now, there's nothing that says you can't get creative with this methodology. For instance, if a spell's goal is augmented by casting it on a Wednesday and today is Sunday, you could substitute a spell component (herbs, stones, colors, candles, or whatever) made or gathered on a Wednesday for the correct timing. This means setting up your magical pantry with a little diligence, taking care to mark all components with labels that show what they are, any metaphysical correspondences, and the Moon phase, astrological sign, month, and hour when that item was made, purchased, or gathered.

Taking this one step farther, think of it this way: magic works outside time and space. So, if a procedure calls for timing it on a Tuesday and it's Monday, you could wait. Or you could recognize that it is Tuesday across the dateline and generate the magic bearing this in mind. Similarly, remember that different parts of the world have different timelines, allowing you a little more flexibility in this arena.

On the following pages you will find simplified charts to get you started thinking in terms of what time is best for your magical proceedings, including more advanced efforts.

ADVANCED WITCHCRAFT

Day	Associations
Monday	Lunar magic, goddess energy
Tuesday	Legal matters, strategy, power
Wednesday	Muse, innovation, visualization
Thursday	Dedication, vitality, success, duty
Friday	Fertility, love, kinship
Saturday	Banishing, destruction
Sunday	Authority, Sun magic, god energy

Daily Cycles	Associations
Daylight	Conscious self, reason, blessings
Darkness	Emotions, introspection, dreams
Dawn	Hope, beginnings, pathworking
Dusk	Endings, completion, transition
Midnight	Spirit conjuring, spirt flight (astral travel)

Month	Associations
January	Safety, passages, protection
February	Well-being, forgiveness, restitution
March	Success, excellence, winning fights
April	Luck, openings, youthful energy
May	Development, advancement, Earth magic
June	Dedication, constancy, love
July	Authority, dignity, self-regulation
August	Peace, accord, symmetry
September	Spiritual attainment, understanding
October	Change, transition
November	Psychism, perception, kindness
December	Wisdom, sensibility, discretion

Moon	Associations
Full	Maturity, completion, fertility
Waxing	Growth, progression, manifestation
Waning	Banishing, turning energy, reducing
Dark	Rest, gestation, cleansing

Next, let's look at the idea of repetition. Repetition is important because it builds sympathetic energy that supports your magical goal. There are several ways to incorporate repetition into magical procedures beneficially, especially rituals and spells. First is the most obvious: that of repeating phrases a specific number of times which mystically corresponds to the goal. A good book on numerology will help you with this, but here's a very general overview:

Number	Associations
1	Self, single-mindedness, solidarity, originality
2	Duality, partnership, accord, balance
3	Triune nature, fortitude, magic, relationships
4	Creation, elemental magic, intention, squaring
5	Psychism, insight, adaptability, the pentagram
6	Completion, protection, devotion, endings
7	Diversity, cycles, perspective
8	Leadership, change, energy, courage, power
9	Service, deeper mysteries, universal standards
10	Judgement, culmination, conscious self
11	Lessons, growth, sharing
12	Attainment, fulfilled cycles, productivity
13	Reverence, pleasant surprises, tolerance

Second, you can commit yourself to repeating a specific spell or ritual regularly for a certain number of days, weeks, months, or even years. This repetitive procedure is often aimed at life-changing goals like breaking addictions, changing long-term negative thought patterns and habits, or creating a positive atmosphere for realizing difficult personal aspirations. Such spells and rituals take tremendous dedication, self-discipline, and focus to maintain over the prespecified duration but the results are well worth it.

To illustrate the concept with a vignette, take a college student whose chosen field is very competitive. This individual might devote their time and energy to a self-designed waxing moon ritual every month until graduation. This ritual would be contrived in such a way that it augments their education and aptitude. It would also include spells, meditations, chants, and the like that would prime the magical pump for career opportunities upon graduation. Consider for a moment how much positive energy twelve or thirteen rituals a year over two to four years' time would generate toward this student's goal!

Exactly what you focus on during successive rituals or spells is wholly up to you. What may seem like a very small or simple thing to someone else can appear overwhelming from where you stand. So, don't feel awkward about giving any difficulty or need in your life this kind of long-term attention. Living the magic also means a willingness to endure, persist, and persevere—never give up on your hopes, your magic, or yourself.

PETS AS FAMILIARS

While the media might equate a black cat or a toad with Witchcraft because of old stereotypes, you don't often see people in the magical community working with physical familiars. Part of the problem comes from housing that doesn't allow pets. The other part is that some of the knowledge of how to effectively find and work with familiars was lost with our ability to commune with the natural world. But since one of the adept's goals is reestablishing this link, working *with* a familiar offers an excellent way to begin.

First comes finding a familiar. Actually, this means voicing a request so a familiar chooses and *finds you*. How do you place this wish before the universe? I suggest going to a natural location with a small offering. Sit down and meditate, visualizing yourself, your home, and your magic in as much detail as possible. Think of this as a spiritual letter of introduction.

After the visualization, mark the offering you've chosen with a little of your own *essence*. Leave it wherever you feel you should. Then go home. Over the next few days, weeks, and even months, keep your eyes and ears spiritually open but try not to have any preconceived notions of what might answer your spiritual call.

While animals such as cats, dogs, and toads were definitely the most prevalent familiars in history and literature, familiars can potentially be plants, too. Just like animals, plants can empathically communicate with humans, and their spirits offer potent lessons with regard to the natural world. So, if you call for a familiar and a sapling suddenly appears near your home, don't automatically dismiss the occurrence. This little sprout could be your answer just as easily as a stray kitten!

Once a familiar finds you, it requires special care and treatment befitting its function as a magical partner. This is no ordinary pet or houseplant. It is a friend and ally. Commune with your familiar as often as possible. Talk to it during feedings or watering. Give it energized tokens like a crystal in its bedding or soil, or blessed name tags.

Make the creature or plant part of your magical studies by having it nearby when you work or read. Bring it into the sacred space, or into any region where you have your magical tools and observe it. Nature's citizens are close to the Mother and generally more sensitive to spiritual energy than we are. Observing and listening closely to the familiar's missives both within and without the circle will often prove very helpful in the days or weeks ahead. Also note that your familiar may try to communicate with you through dreams, since this is a time when humans are naturally more open to psychic input. Keep a dream diary handy just in case!

Learn as much about the animal or plant that has come to you as possible, including proper care, odd characteristics, and the folklore and superstitions behind it. (Two good books for animals are *Animal Speak* by Ted Andrews and *Symbolic & Mythological Animals* by J. C. Cooper.) This allows you to give your familiar proper care. It also honors the familiar's companionship (after all, humans usually make an effort to get to know good friends) and gives you valuable magical information. For example, found cat whiskers are excellent components in wish magic. This knowledge is very handy for someone with a cat familiar. Someone with a rose familiar will find that its petals and leaves, when taken with permission, make terrific additions to love, health, and luck magic—like carrying the rose petal in your wallet for better luck with money, putting it in your shoes so health walks with you, or scattering the rose petals to the wind so love will find you.

Once you know your familiar and its energies intimately, you can then begin working with it regularly in spells and rituals. Animals like dogs and cats will often make their own way into a magical procedure simply by lying down somewhere or walking around. Less mobile animals, like birds, might be placed in the appropriate elemental quarter of the circle to augment that energy (with birds, the East). And as I mentioned previously, familiar plant parts will frequently find their way into magical preparations—these are the plant's gift to you!

The number of ways a familiar augments magic depends much upon the familiar and its chosen partner. My best advice is to be sensitive to your familiar's leadings. Let it guide you in the best ways for the two of you to share sacred space and magical energy. This will be a learning experience that draws you into Mother Earth's educational classroom, which lies directly along the path to adepthood.

SPELLS, CHARMS, AND AMULETS

Spinning spells and creating amulets, charms, and the like are (by my estimation) the two favorite magical techniques used by Witches today. These methods are marvelously quick and easy in comparison to rituals, which make them among the perfect magical vehicles for the busy modern world. But what of the adept factor? How do we advance folk magic to new levels (other than by using a familiar)?

First, begin noting each spell you enact and charm you create alongside its components, incantations, and so forth in a workbook. Write down how you feel after the process is completed. As the magic manifests, detail the time, date, and any oddities in the way the spell or charm terminated. By doing this on a regular basis, you'll discover which types of spells and charms work best for you, which do not, and which ones exhibit unanticipated results.

More important to adept processes, you'll also discover what glitches these magical procedures can suffer due to omissions and oversights. For example, if you omit a specific timeframe from your spell, it might manifest more quickly or slowly than anticipated. Or if you phrase the empowering incantation erroneously in an abundance amulet, you might get flourishing houseplants instead of improved finances.

These kinds of muddled outcomes, which often illustrate the universe's sense of humor, are why I often stress detailing your magical procedures in advance, asking yourself questions like:

- Who or what is the energy aimed toward?
- When does it need to manifest for the best results?
- What specific type of energy do you need to create, and what are the best components to augment this goal?
- Where is the best place to enact this spell, ritual, or whatever (and why)?
- Are all these questions answered and specified in the charm or spell (through words, actions, or symbols)?

One thing that alleviates magical misdirection is to think in more detail about your choices of ingredients for each spell or charm, looking for coherence. Make sure that every object, aroma, action, and word involved in your magical procedure works harmoniously toward your goal. Meticulous attention to minute details produces focused thoughts and therefore highly focused magic.

Another way of augmenting spellcraft and amulet creating is that of creativity and resourcefulness (see Chapter Four). Everything in the world has magical potential if you look with an appreciative spiritual eye. Just because an object or item hasn't been noted in an ancient grimoire as a charm, a spell component, or a ritual tool doesn't mean it can't be used as one!

The ancient magi were very pragmatic—if it was available and meaningful, they used it. So, go ahead and include a paper clip as part of a spell for "connections," or weave some rubber bands together around a magnet as a charm to draw fellow magical associates into your life's "network." In this context, absolutely nothing is silly if you trust in the symbolism and use it reverently.

A third way of advancing spellcraft and amuletic arts is by growing or making the components yourself. Let's use the example of flowers. Plant seeds at auspicious times, separating them in the garden by magical associations. This way the growing, focused energy of one flower improves that of its companions and vice versa. As the flower grows, you can chant to it, sing to it, pray over it, leave small stones in the soil after weeding that augment that flower's energy, and so forth. Finally, you can harvest the flowers when needed for a charm, amulet, or spell, giving thanks to the plant and to Earth for this gift.

A second example can be found in candle magic. Save all your candle ends and pieces from various spells, separated by their magical application and color or aroma associations. Re-melt the bits from any one theme (like love) during an auspicious hour or astrological phase. Stir the wax clockwise to draw in positive energy, blend in harmonious herbs, and then put the whole thing into a mold. After the wax cools, carve it with a symbol suited to the goal at hand (perhaps a heart in this example). I admit that this kind of process takes time and attention but all the while, your personal energy goes into the creation and final product. This means that the candle (or whatever) will be more responsive to you and the magical energy in the sacred space.

Finally, spice up the meaningful energy in spells and charms during the creation process. Say you're putting together an herb bundle for love. Consider the order in which the herbs go into the container so they can build upon one another. You could, for example, begin with an earthy scent or root herb so the relationship has firm foundations. Build on this base with something that symbolizes trust and fidelity. Afterward, add a compassionate aromatic, followed by one for passion. In this manner, your charm is patterned in the same way as most long-term, fulfilling relationships! This particular example would work exceedingly well for a magical love incense, too.

Spells work similarly. If you're releasing ingredients into a wind, combining them, pouring them out, or binding items together, think about:

- *The direction of movement (including up and down).* To get a dream to take to flight, the components should move upward and Easterly for hopefulness. To ground a sickness, you might consider tossing components downward and Westward, downward and counterclockwise, or into a stream flowing away from you.
- *The order and timing of the progression.* For example, in a binding ritual it helps to actually tie or enclose a symbolic item at the same time you're reciting the part of the incantation in which the word *bind* occurs.
- *The position of your body and location in which you cast the spell.* For instance, if you're trying to build a strong foundation beneath a beloved project, do it beneath a tree or sitting close to the earth where roots can take hold.

I think you will find that most of these additions don't excessively increase the amount of time necessary to plan and execute spells and charms. They will, however, improve your overall results. And most important to the adept, these additions encourage new, unique, and exciting dimensions in spellcraft and amuletic arts that shape your insights and the way you will work magic in the future.

Rituals

Adepts hope to make life itself a ritual and an act of worship. How? By the attitude with which they approach each moment. Be that as it may, there are many occasions when even the most advanced practitioner wants something more formalized for honoring the Sacred Powers, commemorating special events, or generating magical energy for specific goals. Ritual offers a functional construct for doing all these things and much more. Inside this construct, your insights, attitudes, awareness, and creativity blossom into the energy of magic.

Some rituals or sections of specific rituals, however, are not designed for novices. For example, in most covens, you'll notice that the Priest or Priestess directs the cone of power. This is also generally the person who participates in rituals of Drawing Down the Moon or Sun, the Great Rite, and calling spirits. Calling spirits is very involved, so I've covered it in detail in Chapter Seven. The remainder of these subjects follow here.

Directing the Cone of Power

Sacred space is like a spiritually protected, three-dimensional bubble. In this confine, dancing, chanting, singing, drumming, clapping, and visualization are all ways that individuals or groups raise energy into raw, distilled willpower with a distinct purpose. Then, as the energy reaches a pinnacle, practitioners fashion it into a specific pattern. This singular thought form bears a shape, color, texture, and movement suited to the goal of the rite.

In your own advanced rituals, all four elements of the cone of power need to be harmonious for long-lasting and accurate results. First, looking to the shape, concentrate on making a figure that symbolizes the goal in your mind's eye while you work. A healing ritual might have a cone of power shaped like a fountain of light; a spring ritual's power might be shaped like a seed of energy that slowly blossoms into a flower.

Next, color this shape with a consonant hue. Returning to our previous examples, green is a good choice in healing, and pastel pink or yellow could be used for spring. Here is a brief color chart to which you can add personal associations

Color	Correspondences
Red	Life's energy, protection, bravery, Fire magic, love, passion
Orange	Harvest of labors, kinship, kindness, attraction
Yellow	Psychism, the mind, communication, Air magic
Green	Abundance, faith, hope, growth, maturity
Blue	Tranquility, truce, joy, Water magic
Purple	Spirituality, higher laws, leadership, dreams
Brown	Grounding, stability, nature, Earth magic
Black	Rest, hidden matters, banishing

Note that your choice of the cone's color may be based on common psychological correspondences for a hue, or on personal experience and emotional impact. For example, blue generates energy for peace and happiness in most people. But if your mother always made you wear blue shirts, it's likely that the only thing this color generates in you is aggravation or resentment. Go with whichever approach works best for you.

The third dimension to the cone of power is texture. The easiest way to decide the best texture for your ritual is by going through your closet and noting how different fabrics make you feel: cozy? Safe? Loved? Empowered? Passionate? If you think of the energy in your cone of power as a finely woven tapestry, then adding the texture from a well-known fabric isn't too difficult. This way, the cone's texture is not simply astral or physical—it's an emotional nap you give to the whole.

Finally comes movement within the cone suited to your intention. In the illustration for a healing ritual, the fountain's water might turn counterclockwise (and even move backward) to symbolically banish illness. For a spring rite, the seed might spin clockwise—the direction of the Sun—until it sprouts and opens fully.

The sacred space's sphere remains in place, holding this "flower" of energy until directed otherwise. Thus, the difficulty for the advanced student is not so much the creation of power as knowing when to guide the cone, and to where. The inexperienced tend to get overly anxious and release the energy before it crests, while someone whose attention wanders might release it late, or guide it only partway out of the circle.

A second difficulty is getting over the temptation to dissipate the energy instead of using it like an arrow. The former often happens unwittingly through loud noises or shouting when people get excited. At this point, it is an adept's role to step in, hold the energy together, and release it properly. Exactly what constitutes a "proper" release, however, depends much upon the goal of the event.

Rituals for individuals need to be guided inward, like a funnel pouring down into the receptacle of self. Rituals for circumstances need to be guided outward to the spiritual event horizon—with that situation constantly in mind—then liberated. Those for Earth should be channeled into the soil, and so forth.

Truth be told, elders in the community have told me that guiding the cone of power isn't easy for them either, especially not in group settings. So, don't get discouraged if you release it at the wrong time or misdirect the energy on several occasions. This is perfectly normal. What's important here is that you continue working with the cone, getting to know how to use your mind and willpower to eventually direct it perfectly. Even at this point, there are bound to be errors generated by any number of circumstances. A covener sneezing, someone coming to the door, or a really annoying itch can all distract from the job at hand. That's part of being human, and it keeps us on our toes!

Drawing Down the Moon

This particular ritual is among the most beautiful in my opinion. During the ritual, an individual evokes and accepts the persona of the Goddess, in all her forms, and actualizes that power in a type of spiritual possession.

Traditionally, a woman performs Drawing Down the Moon because of femininity's links with the Goddess's archetypal power. But what happens when there isn't a woman available for this ritual, or if someone else wants to commune with the Goddess similarly?

While not everyone in Wicca will agree with me, I personally believe anyone can effectively Draw Down the Moon (just as anyone can Draw the Sun). Since each person has lived many lives, usually as different genders, the soul itself knows both the masculine and feminine energies of Creation. Therefore, there is nothing that inhibits a man or nonbinary person from finding the Goddess in themselves if they truly wish it and approach the ritual with respectfulness.

Drawing Down the Moon is considered very holy. It should only be used as preparation for the Great Rite, when a person wishes to connect with the Goddess on a truly intimate level for the purpose of spiritual growth or other urgent needs. The Goddess is maternal, nurturing, healing, intuitive, life-giving, fertile, inspiring, motivational, and emotional; her powers are best called upon for aims suited to these domains (health, productivity, creativity, love, insight, and the like).

What follows here is an original Drawing Down the Moon Ritual that you can try if you feel ready. You will notice that I have not focused on any specific goddess for this rite or for that of Drawing the Sun (invoking the god aspect). While you may certainly adjust these procedures to invoke a specific divine presence, I feel that a true Drawing welcomes the God or Goddess in all forms, no matter the name.

Drawing Down the Moon Ritual

It is imperative that this ritual proceeds without interruptions, so take extra precautions against the phone, pets, children, and potential guests disrupting things. Also, really meditate as to why you wish to enact this rite. You should not perform it just for an interesting spiritual experience or out of curiosity. You will be meeting and uniting with the most sacred of Powers. It is not an undertaking to enter into lightly.

Timing: A Monday night or during a full moon when the Goddess's energy predominates.

Preparations: Fasting for a day beforehand (up to three days, if physically feasible) cleanses the body and prepares it for becoming the temporary temple of the Divine. Take a ritual bath with purifying herbs like thyme, rosemary, mint, and lemon. Also add rose or lily petals, two flowers sacred to many of the world's goddesses. Find music that has Goddess-centered chants or makes you think of her. Higher tones specifically augment Goddess energy, like flutes or small bells.

The Altar: Cover the altar with a white or silver-colored cloth. Have lotus or sandalwood incense burning. A white cup or crystal vase can be used in lieu of a Goddess image if you don't have one (put this in the center of the altar). Place a bowl of flower petals to the right of the chosen image, a white candle in back of it, to represent Spirit, and a candle that will represent you to the left of center. Have a cup of water anywhere on the altar near the front.

The Circle: Since Earth and Water are considered feminine, place special flowers or decorations at the North (a blossoming flower, perhaps) and West (a seashell with a Yoni shape, for example) of the circle. Air and Fire can be represented in any manner customary to your tradition. Use rose water to asperge the sacred space and your own aura. If it helps your focus, put images of strong female role models around the circle to surround yourself with sympathetic energy.

Invocation: Begin in the East, moving clockwise to the quarter points as noted.

> *East:* "Greetings to the Powers of Air. Move into this sacred space with the winds of Spirit and protect all gathered here. Let me breathe in, and become one with, the Goddess, so I might know her voice in myself, others, and the world."

> *South:* "Greetings to the Powers of Fire. Ignite this sacred space with the embers of Spirit and protect all gathered here. Let me be warmed by, and become one with, the Goddess, so I can see her light shining in myself, others, and the world."

West: "*Greetings to the Powers of Water. Flow into this sacred space with the elixir of Spirit and protect all gathered here. Let me drink deeply of, and become one with, the Goddess, so I might feel her wholeness flowing in myself, others, and the world.*"

North: "*Greetings to the Powers of Earth. Root this sacred space in the rich soils of Spirit and protect all gathered here. Let me be enriched by, and become one with, the Goddess, so I can see her blossoming in myself, others, and the world.*"

Center: "*Greetings, great Goddess! She who is, was, and always shall be! Maiden, Mother, Crone, come! Be welcome here and bless our efforts in this sacred space. So mote it be.*"

Light the spirit candle on the altar to signal the Goddess's presence and sprinkle her flower petals liberally around the base. Stay in the center of the room (if working alone) or sit in a circle (if working with a group) for the meditation.

Meditation: See yourself as you sit now. Above you is a radiant silver-white light pouring down. This light has a face so beautiful and potent you can barely look at it. It is the Goddess, young and lovely yet ancient and wise. Her face shifts into feminine images from many cultures, some old, some young… then the pictures fade back to blazing, energizing light.

As the light shines down, it begins to saturate your crown chakra, then spreads throughout your body. Feel the Goddess's power as it cleanses and renews you from head to toe.

At last, the light will come to rest in your heart chakra. You can feel part of the Goddess within you, uniting with that without, and blossoming. Focus on this wholly. Welcome the Goddess who is already part of you. (Note: if you're doing the drawing yourself, you should hold this image and move to the altar at this point. Otherwise, everyone should direct the Goddess energy to the person who will be Drawing Down the Moon.)

Drawing: During the drawing, the person becoming the Goddess should light their personal candle off the Spirit candle and kneel before the altar, the seat of Spirit. Some people find it helpful to dance clockwise around the sacred space first to bring forth a trancelike state; others chant, intone mantras, or meditate. You will have to find out what metaphysical approach brings you to the deepest state of altered awareness and use this.

As you feel yourself slipping into the astral and the world around fading, welcome the Goddess by raising your hands to embrace her. Give yourself wholly to her. Feel the Ancient Mother who gave all things life return your embrace and gather you into her heart. Move aside your ego and relinquish control of your body and mind temporarily to her power. Let go and let her guide what happens next. Don't be afraid. You'll still be there as a copilot. Besides, the Goddess is always a good houseguest. She leaves when asked.

Activities: Much depends on the purpose for this ritual. The living Goddess may do healing work, divine the future, offer motherly advice, guide a creative exercise, and so forth. In the case of a ritual for personal growth and deeper understanding of the Goddess, she will likely simply commune with you. Generally speaking, it's best not to plan out this part of the ritual in advance—the Goddess has her own agenda and will provide a delightful surprise suited to the occasion.

Release: When you feel the Goddess's activities are ending (trust me when I say you will simply know this), return to kneeling before the altar. Lift your hands high again but this time in release. Move back away from the Mother's embrace and thank her silently as you go. Slowly adjust your breathing to a normal pace, blow out the Spirit candle to represent the Goddess's release, and drink the glass of water before closing the circle.

Closing: Dismiss the quarters in a manner suited to your tradition, adding a final prayer like this one for closure:

> *"Great Goddess, (my/our) thanks to you for spending time with us in the physical realm. I will cherish your wisdom and insights, carrying them in my heart. As I go from this place, help me to ever remember that you are always part of me, and the world—in the Moon, in the waters, in my life's blood, and most important in my spirit. So be it."*

DRAWING DOWN THE SUN

Drawing Down the Sun is, as might be expected, very similar to Drawing Down the Moon other than its timing and key symbolic components. In this case, you will be uniting with the sacred masculine energies: the God self, which, like the Goddess, is available to everyone no matter their gender. As with Drawing Down the Moon, this ritual should be enacted for important goals suited to the God's traditional spheres: leadership, the conscious mind, strength, courage, questing, blessing, hope, protection, illumination, power, victory in battles, and the like.

Timing: Sunday or at noon, when the God's power is strongest.

Advanced Witchcraft

Preparations: Similar to those for Drawing Down the Moon, except that you should add musky or spicy masculine scents (like patchouli and allspice) to your bathwater to accent God energies. Also, change the music to drumming or strong bass instrumentals—sounds that reflect the deeper-toned male voice.

The Altar: Cover the altar with a yellow or gold-colored cloth. Have dragon's blood, cedar, or mint incense burning. A phallus or rectangular stone can be used in lieu of a God image if you don't have one (put this in the center of the altar). Place a bowl of seeds to the right of the chosen image, a white candle behind it to represent Spirit, and a candle that will represent you to the left of center. Have a cup of water anywhere on the surface near the front.

The Circle: Since Air and Fire are considered masculine elements, place special decorations at the South (a red candle) and East (two nuts) of the circle. Earth and Water can be represented in any manner customary to your tradition. Use pine water to asperge the sacred space and your own aura. If it helps your focus, put images of strong male role models around the circle to surround yourself *with* sympathetic energy.

Invocation: Begin in the East, moving clockwise to the quarter points as noted.

> *East:* "Greetings to the Powers of Air. Move into this sacred space with the winds of Spirit and protect all gathered here. Let me breathe in, and become one with, the God, so I might know his voice in myself, others, and the world."

South: "Greetings to the Powers of Fire. Ignite this sacred space with the embers of Spirit and protect all gathered here. Let me be impassioned by, and become one with, the God, so I can see his sacred flame burning in myself, others, and the world."

West: "Greetings to the Powers of Water. Flow into this sacred space with the elixir of Spirit and protect all gathered here. Let me drink deeply of, and become one with, the God, so I might feel his power cresting in myself, others, and the world."

North: "Greetings to the Powers of Earth. Root this sacred space in the rich soils of Spirit and protect all gathered here. Let me be strengthened by, and become one with, the God, so I can see his sacred seed in myself, others, and the world."

Center: "Greetings, great God! He who is, was, and always shall be! Son, Father, Grandfather, come! Be welcome here and bless our efforts in this sacred space. So mote it be."

Light the candle central to the altar to signal the God's presence and sprinkle his seed liberally around the base. Stay in the center of the room (if working alone) or move into a circle (if working with a group) for the meditation.

Meditation: See yourself as you sit now. Above you is a radiant gold-yellow light pouring down. This light has a face so strong and powerful, you can barely look at it. It is the God, young and energetic, yet ancient and discerning. His face shifts into masculine images from many cultures, some old, some young...then the pictures fade back to blazing, energizing light.

As the light shines down, it begins to saturate your crown chakra, then spreads throughout your body. Feel the God's power as it purifies and energizes you from head to toe. At last, the light will come to rest in your heart chakra. You can feel part of the God within you uniting with that without and sparking into a flame. Focus on this wholly. Welcome the God who is already part of you. (Note: if you're doing the drawing yourself, you should hold this image and move to the altar at this point. Otherwise, everyone should direct the God energy to the person who will be Drawing Down the Sun.)

Drawing: During the drawing, the person becoming the God should light their personal candle from that of Spirit, and kneel before the altar, the seat of Spirit. Some people find it helpful to dance clockwise around the sacred space first to engender a trancelike state; others chant, intone mantras, or meditate. You will have to find out what metaphysical approach brings you to the deepest state of altered awareness and use this.

As you feel yourself slipping into the astral and the world around fading, welcome the God. Raise your hands to the heavens and give yourself wholly to him. Feel the Ancient Father welcome you back to his side, then gather you into his heart. Move aside your ego and relinquish control of your body and mind temporarily to his power. Let go and let him guide what happens next. As with Drawing Down the Moon, you'll find the God is as considerate with your body, if not more so, than you would be. You have nothing to fear.

Activities: Much depends on the purpose for this ritual. The living God may perform a blessing, channel energy and health, offer logical insights, guide an illuminating exercise, and so on. Don't try to plan this part of the ritual in advance—the God, like the Goddess, knows what we need and will provide it in a unique way.

Release: When you feel the God's activities are ending, return to kneeling before the altar. Lift your hands high again but this time in release. Move back away from the Father's embrace and thank him silently as you go. Slowly adjust your breathing to a normal pace, blow out the Spirit candle, and drink the glass of water before closing the circle.

Closing: Use any traditional circle banishing you like, adding a prayer like this one for closure:

> *"Great God, (my/our) thanks to you for spending time with us in the physical realm. I will cherish your strength and reasoning, carrying them in my heart. As I go from this place, help me to ever remember that you are always part of me, and the world—in the Sun, in the volcanoes, in my life's blood, and most important in my spirit. So be it."*

The Great Rite

The Great Rite symbolizes the sacred marriage between Heaven and Earth, God and Goddess, and Spirit and matter. In ancient times, this was a rite that culminated in copulation, the ultimate life-giving act that releases tremendous energy. Today, symbolic tacks are often chosen instead for many reasons, including physical safety and social propriety. This symbolic approach is used here with the knowledge that an emblem, within the magic circle, is just as powerful as what it represents—as long as it's treated with similar reverence.

The Great Rite is generally reserved for times of great need (like famines, drought, and plagues), when a balancing and union of the greatest powers in the universe are required for speedy manifestation. Please note that this sample ritual is written for the solitary Witch but can be modified for group practice.

Timing: Often need-specific, but dawn, dusk, midnight, during eclipses and equinoxes, and other "in-between" hours are a good choice, when light and dark, sounds and silences, are in balance. This gives the dualistic powers of the universe equivalent symbolic expression.

Preparations: Similar to those for Drawing. Fast, pray, bathe, and carefully ponder the reasons you're doing this. Many people prefer to enact the Great Rite skyclad so no worldly illusions affect the ritual.

The Altar: Include a God and Goddess image (if possible, embracing or very close to one another) and equal amounts of lunar and solar symbolism. Try a white and yellow candle for Spirit, a blend of carrot and tomato juice for the ritual cup, ginger and vanilla incense, a deep chalice, and a wand or dagger.

The Circle: Sprinkle rose petals and rosemary around the perimeter of the circle. Asperge the sacred space with an infusion made from lemon. Mark the quarter points in any manner suited to your tradition. Try to balance the amount of light and darkness coming into the room.

Invocation: Again, this may be anything traditional, with the addition of a prayer (like this one) that indicates your intention:

> "Lady and Lord, join me in this place beyond space and time. I welcome you. Today I celebrate you as a

> *whole being, neither male nor female but the best of both. Within this union all things in the universe were made, and to it all things shall return. Come, now, and bless this effort. Bring me (describe the need or reason that you're enacting the rite)."*

Meditation: See yourself as you stand right now in your mind's eye. Above you is a glowing yin-yang symbol; one half is colored silver and the other half is gold. The light is brilliant, refreshing, and inviting. Reach your arms upward to embrace it and pull the symbol into yourself. (Note: you can pull it into any part of your body, but many people prefer putting it near the womb or loins to represent the generative forces of life.)

As the light settles into your being, notice how balanced and symmetrical it is. There is no pushing or pulling—no weakness in being intuitive and no greatness implied by rationality. Both are important, and both are part of you and the divine. Take as long as you need to focus on the dichotomy of the God and Goddess united yet retaining their individuality. Think about this polarity in yourself and welcome both halves as part of your wholeness.

When you can feel this creative, generative force reaching a peak, open your eyes and continue with the ritual.

The Rite: Hold the cup in one hand and your athame or wand in the other. Slowly lower the athame and point it down into the chalice to symbolize the union of opposites, saying:

> *"Let your powers combine for the sacred dance that began Creation. In this moment, the God and Goddess are of one mind, one heart, one spirit…working together for (describe your need or goal). May your wisdom and power lodge where most needed for the greatest good, and harm none."*

Activities: Spells, incantations, chants, dances, and the like specifically designed to amplify energy for your need or goal. If there is any way you can keep the chalice and knife or wand together during this time, I recommend it.

Closing: Slowly remove the wand or dagger from the cup; if it's already removed, simply hold one in each hand.

Personal Dynamics

All in all, elevating traditional methods is not really about a step upward but one outward and inward. It's about expanding the way you perceive yourself, the world, and the universe of magic. Release yourself to broaden those horizons, then move forward, making magic a true art—the art of the adept.

CHAPTER FOUR

MAGICAL ARTISTRY

"Perfection consists not in doing extraordinary things, but in doing ordinary things extraordinarily well."
—Marie Angélique Arnauld

Magic is an art, which means that it takes time to develop your personal voice to the point where everything comes together and works. It also means that, just as with any creative endeavor, there is more than one school of magical arts. These schools aren't institutions as we think of for traditional education. Instead, an adept's early training comes from individuals and small groups who share a heritage and the methods that they've learned, rather like an apprenticeship program.

For example, the school of folk magic teaches well-known superstitions as a familiar foundation for generating positive energy. The High Magician's academy uses intricate ritual similarly. In the Kitchen Witch's classroom, we find people blending together components found in, and around, the sacred space of home for spellcraft. The Dianic school directs a large part of its curriculum toward feminine issues and the Goddess.

Each school or style has its own merit, and each expresses a unique spiritual vision suited to its practitioners. Nonetheless, even within this brief overview of magical schools—there are many more—some basic differences in ideology and approach are evident. You will need to consider these variations in determining the best, most meaningful way to make your magic an art form.

One major consideration is deciding between tradition and innovation, or a combination thereof. For example, High Magic leans very heavily on tradition, following rituals from long ago, believing that repetition and exactness improve each ritual's results. Mind you, High Magicians frequently work with spirits, which requires a solid, successful, and safe construct.

Meanwhile, a folk magician like me often wings it, using gut instinct as a guiding force for manifesting power. Does this mean that a folk magician's innovative approach requires any less skill? Absolutely not. In order to effectively bring novelty to their art, folk magicians must be conversant and proficient in several magical techniques. This way they can decide which approach is best considering the goal, the surroundings, relevant folklore, and the components or tools available.

Blending these two schools together makes for some wonderful rituals and spells. In this case, tradition provides the black-and-white outlines for the adept, and creativity colors them in! The advantage of this particular mixture is that it allows us to honor our history, add personal vision, and leave room for Spirit to inspire unscripted words or actions.

This brings me to the second major consideration: complexity versus simplicity. In a world where fancy often means better, magic has no such restrictions. A simple, heartfelt ritual can be just as empowering and transformational as a detailed, three-hour ceremony. What makes the difference? The skill, will, faith, and focus of the magician (or group). Both approaches have advantages and drawbacks.

A *complex* spell, ritual, meditation, or whatever adds sensual and spiritual dimensions to the working. Each portion is carefully designed to increase or direct energy. On the other hand, it's easy to forget parts of a highly detailed procedure, or to lose people's attention during it. Similarly, too much focus on the details can manifest a heady ritual or spell, instead of one that pours from the heart and spirit.

The *simple* spell, ritual, meditation, or whatever provides magicians with more time to focus on their magical intention instead of minute details. In a busy world filled with multitasking, simple folk magics offer a fairly quick means of spiritually augmenting a goal. On the other hand, it's tempting to get mentally sloppy or lazy with uncomplicated approaches. Think of this as akin to the difference between how you feel wearing sweatpants and wearing a three-piece suit. And thanks to our societal training, it's also tempting to subconsciously doubt the validity of something that seems easy. Intuitive, natural processes should flow effortlessly!

Consideration three is whether to focus on one aspect of the God, Goddess, or a differently gendered deity, or to trust the Universal All to carefully steer your magic once it's past the spiritual event horizon. The answer to this quandary really lies in your ideas about how magic and the universe work. Not every adept worships a god or goddess, but most acknowledge a force behind Creation—an energy source where the strands of magic originate along with all life.

I personally think that in our progression toward advanced methods, we need to balance the yin-yang energies within ourselves and come to know both aspects of the One. Our learning cannot be complete otherwise. In a very broad sense, to know only the God brings sunshine, reason, and hope, but no intuition or feeling. Similarly, to know only the Goddess brings moonlight, dreams, and insight, but no might or warrior instincts. By knowing both and reuniting with these powers, we find the fount of the universe that flows within and without all things. Here are the waters of magic!

Bearing all this in mind, part of magical artistry is finding just the right blend and balance of tradition, innovation, complexity, simplicity, God, and Goddess that really expresses who you are as a spiritual being. Like any great masterpiece, it will take time and experimentation to discover this harmonious blend. But the trial-and-error approach is much easier when you bear in mind that *you* are the work-in-progress and your magic is the paint.

MAGICAL MUSE

No matter the school or style, adepts are truly artists in their own right. Each line and curve of the magical energy they create has meaning and power. Better still, there are many arts and crafts that lend themselves to adepts' magical inventiveness very nicely. How? By manifesting energy through the creation process.

Think of it this way: as a lyricist writes a song, each line builds upon the story created by the last. The end result is a complete view of what the songwriter was trying to express. Now put this idea into a magical construct. In this case, the lyrics have spiritual meaning and a specific goal. By the end of the song, the words reflect attainment, thereby generating positive, motivational energy for manifesting the magic!

Try some of the artistic methods that follow to see if any help you express your path and augment your magic.

Word Power

According to biblical tradition, YHWH created with words. Several other gods and goddesses around the world also manifested life's energy by speaking willfully. Since an adept's goal is to return to oneness with this ancient power, they too must learn to wield words with potency.

In the aforementioned example, the lyricist wove magic into words to manifest energy. This illustration is particularly powerful because it returns to the ancient bardic and oral traditions, both of which had mystical overtones. But word power in magic is not limited to songwriting or poetry. It includes the presentation of our everyday speech, incantations, chants, mantras, and written charms. It also includes those conversations we have with ourselves internally—the words within our thoughts.

A creative turn of a phrase backed by meaningful symbolism and a focused will can have amazing results. Daily affirmations are an excellent modern example of this, as are phrases like "from your lips to God's ears." Daily affirmations resonate positive ideas into our aura, which eventually translates this energy into a mental, physical, or spiritual reality. In other words, you are what you think! Similarly, expressing goodwill or wishes, with which others agree, creates a geometric progression of positive power. The possibilities are nearly endless.

Here are some hints to help you integrate word power in daily magic:

- Pay attention to those times when negativity creeps into your thoughts and try to control it. Redirect your attention to something more positive and spiritually fulfilling.

- Watch your words (you might have to eat them later). The way we talk about ourselves can affect magic greatly. For example, a person who puts themselves down is not going to achieve the same level of magical proficiency as a self-confident person. Surety and purpose support magic.
- Find ways to think about your magic whenever possible. Each time you direct thoughts toward a previously enacted spell, ritual, or whatever, you give it more energy with which to manifest.
- Look at what you write and how you write it. In your book of shadows, for example, CAPITALS might be used to stress a goal or represent growth, small lettering could be used to emphasize diminishment or banishing.
- Write a charm for peace and tranquility in blue ink, and one for energy or power in red crayon. Get creative!

Music

It is no accident that music appears as part of religious rituals around the world. Music transports listeners to a different emotional and mental space where they are more open to Spirit's input. For magical musicians, however, music is a way to commune with the Divine and then channel the feelings or messages they receive.

The result improves the ambience of any sacred space, including that special spot in participants' hearts. How? A sensitive drummer slowly increases or decreases the music's pace along with the cresting and waning energy within a circle. An impassioned singer can move listeners to feel and imagine the magical imagery in a song. A guitar player might invent a little tune as the circle progresses with notes reflective of emotions.

The instrument of choice makes little difference here—if you can't sing or drum, try whistling, playing a harmonica, or even rapping rhythmic spoons! Even if you don't consider yourself musically inclined, the God/dess really doesn't care if you're off tune. What's most important is that the instrument and the music uplift your spirit, inspire deeper spiritual states, and offer a creative outlet for your magic. Make a joyful noise!

Dance and Pantomime

Where there's music, dance often follows. King David danced before God in joy and worship. The Dancing Dervishes used dance to generate ecstatic states from which they divined the future. Many ancient religious systems believed that sacred dancing allowed the dancer to commune with the Divine. In Wicca specifically, clockwise dancing accompanies rituals for positive, growth-oriented energy. Counterclockwise dancing accents banishing, turning, or reduction.

Sometimes a sacred dance (like hula) tells a story that mirrors the goal or theme of the rite. Other times, a dance creates a cone of power through its energetic outpouring. But in almost all cases, sacred dancing generates a trancelike state that transports the dancers into an astral realm where they can dance before and with the God/dess.

As with music, you don't have to dance like Fred Astaire. Simple side steps, cross stepping, small jumps, or strides all work well within the magic circle. In fact, you don't need to worry about using any specific steps for the dancing to be effective. I've seen some wheelchair-bound people swing rhythmically in their chairs and attain amazingly deep spiritual states just as well as folks on two feet!

Pantomime is a slightly different tack that combines a dancelike quality with theatrical flair (in some instances, dance includes mimed actions for visual effect). Through the actions of the pantomime, imaginative spellcasters create sympathetic energy for activating their magic. For example, a person performing a spell for love might mimic receiving a hug as part of the procedure. Someone using magic to help with house hunting might mime opening a door to likewise open the right physical doors in meeting this goal.

As you can see in the above examples, generally magical mimicry acts out a spell's or ritual's aim as if it were already manifested. Effectively, this is a kind of imitative magic in which the mime visually weaves the goal into real form, here and now. From a symbolic standpoint, the person's ambition is fulfilled, which makes for a strong subconscious belief that the magic will come to pass.

The nice thing about pantomime is that it's something we all do to some degree. How often have you communicated ideas nonverbally to someone on the phone so as to not interrupt the conversation? This is a simple type of pantomime. For those who know sign language (specifically American Sign Language), it too has pantomime qualities but in this case, words and sentences are given visual form for manifesting your magic!

Domestic Arts

When you're washing the dinner dishes, the idea of domesticity might seem anything but magical. Nonetheless, many traditional domestic chores were historically very artistic in their own right. Believe me when I say it took a creative person to make food for three people stretch to feed six or whip up a healthy elixir from whatever pantry herbs were on hand. And while most people wouldn't have considered their work magical, many cooks up to a hundred years ago could still be found stirring food clockwise or baking bread by a waxing moon for the best, healthiest results!

While times have changed, the creative potential inherent in domestic arts has not. We can still "cook up" power to perfection through any number of methods, not the least of which is mealtime magic. For Kitchen Witches in particular, cookery, brewing, and herbalism remain well-beloved arts for magical expression because of their familiarity and ease of daily integration. For example, put some mystical bubbles into your brews by chanting or singing to them. Blend energy into broths via blessed ingredients. Stitch love into a child's coat when mending it, binding the magic with a knot. Press out problems when ironing your clothes through visualization. Arrange flowers so they're visually appealing and spiritually meaningful, and perhaps even design your home using metaphysical systems like feng shui.

Using domestic artistry to depict and augment your spiritual practices has a wonderful benefit. It emphasizes your body and home as sacred spaces within which positive magic finds daily expression. This expression aids in the adept's goal of living the magic—or at least living *in* it!

HANDCRAFTS

Many people enjoy some type of home handcraft these days, from decoupage and macramé to still-life design and crocheting. All of these arts have magical potential for expressing metaphysical principles. They can also portray the goal of a spell in the way the item is put together or completed.

Consider a collage for family unity as an example. Find pictures that you like of each person in the family (those that show happy, healthy people, especially if they were taken near your home). Hold them together while praying to your household god or goddess for harmony. Glue them on the surface to adhere the magic. This also symbolizes your family "sticking" together. Coat the collage with art spray to protect your family from outside influences. Then, each time you see the collage after it's completed, have an incantation prepared and repeat it verbally or mentally to continue empowering that goal. (Perhaps, *"Unity be with us. Unity flow through us. Our family bind together using love as a tether."*)

Another good example exists in nearly any type of needlecraft. In the Middle East and other parts of the world, knot magic is very popular. By adding an incantation and a little love to a woven rug, fishing net, or scarf, the maker can endow the recipient with comfort, providence, and health, respectively. Taking this idea one step farther, the comfort rug might be woven in shades of blue for joy and peace, the fishing net in gold-toned rope for prosperity, and the scarf in red and green for vitality and healing.

You can also add magical patterns to the mix, like a peace sign on the rug, a square knot in the net (for Earth's abundance), and protective emblems in the scarf. So, take a second look at any handcraft you enjoy to see how you might design the components, colors, and patterns together for any magical goal you hope to achieve, or to instill special energy in a gift for family members and friends.

Painting and Drawing

Like handcrafts, painting and drawing allow you to portray your magical vision and goals in progressive steps. Painters often sketch their work first, symbolically creating a blueprint for the energy to follow. Color, texture, and layering follow, adding life, dimension, and emphasis to specific spiritual areas of the work. For example, a painting of a personal god or goddess might use a predominant color sacred to this Being, textural qualities in the clothing or surroundings to accent the attributes of the Being, and extra layers of white paint around the persona to emphasize the divine light.

In drawing, one line connects to the next, just as our magical lines of energy connect us each to each. While drawings don't allow for layering, per se, the pressure used on the pencil or pen can emphasize light, darkness, emotion, depth, grain and nap, and many other subtle things. So, if you were to create a drawing to help banish a negative habit, the habit might appear very dark and heavy on the left side of a work. As the picture progresses, though, this habit slowly disappears into light, positive imagery on the right. In its finished form, this drawing will have the same effect as diminishing charms of old, like the *Abracadabra* spell!

Paintings and drawings can both be made in various sizes to match the need at hand. Make something large that you can use as a meditative focus. Medium-sized pieces can decorate the sacred space of home, emphasizing your spiritual ambitions each time you see them. Small pieces become portable charms and amulets that tuck neatly into pockets, shoes, purses, or wallets so you can carry the magic wherever you go!

Sculpting and Carving

These are exceptionally fun arts that most people can learn to some degree of proficiency. Even I, Miss Clumsy herself, have managed to become fairly adept at carving soapstone using files. I have a tremendous amount of hope for more coordinated people!

Looking at some specific media, modeling clay is one with a particularly high potential for magic. For adaptable intentions, use the non-hardening type in a color suited to your goal. If you like, add some harmonious oils so you get the added benefit of aromatherapy while you work. For things that require solid, concrete outcomes, use hardening clay; as the figurine solidifies, so does the magic!

Wood carving is a little more difficult but in simple forms it can be used for making magical wands. Consider the type of wood first—for what kinds of magic is it best applied? Next, find tiny crystals that have similar metaphysical correspondences. Carve out small holes, while focusing on the theme of your wand, and adhere the crystals with glue and herbs. Finally, condition the wand with lemon oil to which other appropriate essential oils have been added. Then, in lieu of an athame, you can use this wand to direct your magical energy in any spell or ritual along its theme.

Stone carving does require more elaborate tools. But if you work with soapstone (as I have), all you'll need are some good files and sandpaper to shape your magic. Use any tool with a point to etch out a pattern on a flat side of the stone, dip this in ink, then use it to mark your magical goods like a signature block! Or you can make a rough shape of something you want banished, then file it neatly away.

Don't throw away the debris from this effort. It makes very soft body powder that can also be scented to correspond with magical goals. Add some cinnamon to the powder and put it in your shoes for luck or add powdered roses and rose oil and put it over your heart chakra to draw love into your life.

There are many other arts and crafts that could be used to augment the Adept's Path, but space constraints don't allow for a more detailed review. Go to some art galleries, stop at a store that specializes in past-time supplies, and review books at the library for ideas. With a little effort, you'll find an artistic expression just right for your spiritual ideals and the Adept's Path.

MAZES AND LABYRINTHS

A *maze* is "an intricate winding and turning; a perplexed state of things; and the act of pondering over something deeply. Meanwhile, a labyrinth is "an elaborate path that leads from an entrance to a central point of a garden or other feature" (like a building). By blending these two definitions, we begin to understand the magical art of maze making and walking.

Specifically, a maze maker intuitively creates a large mystical pattern that reflects a question or a topic for meditation. The exact pattern depends largely on the maze's goal, but it needs to be big enough, and sturdy enough, for people to comfortably walk along the finished design. For example, concentric, twisting squares might be painted in browns or greens on a fourteen-foot-square piece of art paper or cardboard, and then used for pondering your spiritual roots or better understanding the elements.

Generally speaking, maze meditations begin on the outer edge of the pattern (representing a genesis or question) and slowly move toward the heart of the matter (the conclusion or answer). A maze designed for banishing, however, may reverse this process for symbolic value. In this case, the walker might start at the core and work outward counterclockwise, to change the negative tendencies.

To get ideas for good maze designs, look at children's puzzles books. In "start here" maze designs, the child has to find their way through from one designated point to another without doubling back or meeting a wall. Many of the patterns featured in these games will actually work on a large scale for magical goals. Here are some basic shape correspondences to consider in looking over pre-made labyrinths:

- *Square and rectangle:* Foundations, security, Earth magic, elemental magic, propriety, motivation, focus, reconciliations
- *Circle:* Cycles, the Moon (silver) or Sun (gold), protection, the soul's eternal nature, reincarnation, making turns for the better
- *Triangle:* The triune nature of the Divine and humankind, unity, meditation, stability (but not as concrete as a square)
- *Pentacle or star:* The forces of magic in balance and cooperation, safety, hope, occult studies, mysticism, calling spirits
- *Tree:* Growth, progress, broadening horizons, the kabbalistic tradition, the Adept's Path

There are obviously many other shapes and shape combinations that you can use in making magical mazes. Meditate on your goal before trying to design one. What are the first shapes you think of? These should be foundational to the maze. The twists and turns are best inspired by Spirit. Try sketching out the design from a trance state, allowing your guides and higher self to lead your hand.

In sharing a finished maze with others, you can tell people what the maze represents or not. Knowing beforehand can help the participants focus on specific goals. On the other hand, seeing what they discern during the walking process can be very revealing. The maze is the shape of magic—the walking creates energy, and in the end what each person takes home will be exactly what they most need from that energized form.

GLAMOURY

"There was the door to which I found no key;
There was the veil through which I might not see."
          —Omar Khayyam

Glamoury is a unique magical art that specializes in illusion. From a mythological standpoint, Witches learned the art of glamoury (or at the very least got some pointers on it) from the fairy-folk, who are incredibly adept at mirages, secrets, and chimerical escapades. Unlike the fey, however, Witches probably shouldn't use glamoury to purposely distort the truth or fool someone into making a bad decision, but to each their own.

Instead, the adept art of glamoury creates a temporary energy facade that goes into place as a coping mechanism, for protection, to improve self-confidence, and other similar purposes. The best way to describe glamoury is as an energy shift in a person's or object's auric field. Visualize this like snowflakes of light and color that swirl, generating a surface upon which images appear rather like a movie screen. The image isn't real, and it doesn't last, but for a while it *seems* real.

Just as a stage illusionist shifts the audience's attention to keep them from seeing what's really taking place, the glamourist uses energy to shift attention and appearances. Here are several examples.

Beauty Booster

Whether other people know it or not, their reactions to you are strongly influenced by interactions with your aura. If glamourists add a little glitz to the formula for magnetic appeal, it makes them more attractive from the inside out. The traditional color for passion and love is red, so the visualization might include red-colored light shaped like hearts dancing in the auric field. This energy then reaches out to potentially positive mates and companions to catch their attention. Better still, since this type of glamoury only boosts what a person already truly is, there's no falsehood involved. As the old saying goes: accent the positive!

Invisibility Aura

Feeling overexposed at work? Wish that you could just disappear in uncomfortable social situations? Glamoury helps with both types of goals. In this instance, put neutral tones (especially gray or blue gray) into your aura to create an astral blue-screen effect. Once this is in place, people may know you're there but for some odd reason they don't really pay that much attention. Similarly, since auric energy has a presence in the astral, spirits won't notice you as readily either!

This invisibility aura is great for moments when you want some temporal or spiritual peace, or when you need to focus without annoying interruptions. Try donning it before balancing your checkbook, studying your book of shadows, or working a difficult spell or ritual. Just remember to remove the energy wrappings when you're done.

Safe Camouflage

This is similar to the aura of invisibility with one minor change. Instead of making yourself disappear, you use color and light to blend yourself or an object into the surroundings. For this, think of the auric field as textural, like paint, and picture yourself slowly merging and harmonizing with the textures around you. This technique is especially useful for large objects, like a home, experiencing psychic attacks. The overall effect is similar to that of the behavior of a chameleon:

the object becomes one with everything around it so that nothing stands out and nothing's out of the ordinary to attract attention from unwanted sources.

Another good use for safe camouflage is protecting costly possessions at home or abroad. For example, wrap your jewelry in the camouflaged aura so that any would-be thief won't notice it. Similarly, wrap your wallet when visiting tourist attractions. Just be aware that you can leave "holes" in the safe camouflage that will let the spirits and people you trust inside the sphere.

Pseudo-Persona

The pseudo-persona should be donned cautiously. It is not appropriate to put on a pseudo-persona for meetings with loved ones; these are people with whom truth and verity are valuable. On the other hand, when life hands you a situation in which you need a different demeanor than normal or a different way of handling things, the pseudo-persona is a perfect coping mechanism.

For example, many Pagans would find themselves uncomfortable as used-car salespeople simply because of this profession's reputation for falsehood. (No offense to the honest used-car salespeople out there.) Yet if this is the only job around to put food on the table, you have a quandary. How do you handle the negative stereotype in a positive, salary-producing manner? In this case, you might sprinkle the attributes of an honest salesperson into your aura (perhaps envisioned as tiny yellow mouths for communication) and something else for money (like miniature gold coins). Afterward, your interactions will carry this welcoming, trustworthy energy to customers—and they will respond to it by buying!

As with most glamoury, please remember to remove this persona once it's no longer needed, like at the end of the day.

The people you care about want to see the real you, not a mirage. Also, stop using it once you've gained the necessary confidence in your own ability to handle a situation without magical assistance. Glamoury is meant to be a short-term helpmate, not a permanent crutch.

With time and diligent practice, glamoury makes a useful and effective add-on to many metaphysical procedures. For example, place silver spheres of light in your aura before Drawing Down the Moon so your physical energy field is already prepared for the Goddess. Or when you cast a spell to speed healing to a part of your body, you might create an energy sphere around that part that is smooth and whole. No matter the magical task at hand, just put on your "glamourous" cloak of magical energy and begin!

Shapeshifting

In shapeshifting, you create yourself in another image, be it that of an animal, plant, mineral, or another person. In many ways, shapeshifting resembles glamoury with a different focal point and overall effect. In this case, the procedure transforms *your* outlook, perceptions, and understanding, not necessarily the way others perceive you.

Although talented shapeshifters can elicit some interesting reactions from the people around them, this isn't the main reason for transfiguration. Instead, the purpose for shapeshifting is to quite literally walk a mile in someone or something else's shoes. This experience allows you to gain deeper comprehension of, and a connection to, various forces in nature, yourself, others, and magic.

Through this technique, you can come to know what it is to fly like a bird (for perspective), run like a wolf (for cunning), watch the world's history like a rock (for patience), or see yourself through a friend's eyes (for clearer discernment). You can travel into a flame and become one with dancing salamanders for joy and energy, vanish into a gust of wind with sylphs to release your inner child and creativity, perhaps even root yourself into a great oak tree to receive strength, or blossom with a Beltane flower to awaken your inner beauty—and that's just a few examples!

The easiest way to comprehend shape shifting is from the spiritual dimension. While the focus of your effort is generally Earth-side, the effect takes place in the astral. Think of it as a sacred communion in which you mold your aura into the image of the thing or person you're honoring. You can do this through visualization, chanting, meditation—any metaphysical technique that works for you. Most people report they experience success by combining careful scrutiny of the item or person with fasting, visualization, glamoury, and meditation.

Like all things in the universe, we are in a constant state of change. Every thought and action changes us inside and out. For example, when we drink water it becomes part of us, along with whatever is in that water. This internalization represents a change and nourishing. Shape shifting simply works with this ongoing transformative energy for more specific purposes.

So, the first question in shapeshifting is either: *what* or *who*? Is there someone you need to better understand? Is there an herb you work with regularly that you'd like more insight into? Do you have an affinity for a particular animal and want to learn more from this creature? The possibilities are as vast and limitless as the universe's wonders and your imagination! Begin by taking these basic steps:

Study your model with an artist's eye. Get to know every line and curve of it. If it's an animal, plant, or stone, research its folklore, preferred habitat, and so forth. The more you know about the prototype, the easier it is to replicate.

Prepare yourself. Take a bath or shower to cleanse your body and smooth your aura. If physically and routinely feasible, spend a day beforehand fasting, praying, reading, and meditating.

Try to get your mind off other matters. You want to be wholly focused on your model and its characteristics.

Add as much sensual input as possible. If the model has an aroma, texture, sound, or whatever, try to have this surrounding you. This way you can build your aura into a new image one dimension at a time.

Release self-images and stop thinking in the physical. Your spirit is not limited by the body's structure. Also, release your expectations; let change happen of its own accord. Give yourself to your inherent magical instincts; give yourself over to the thing or person into which you wish to transform.

Begin visualizing the transformation in successive, slow steps. If it helps, prerecord a guided visualization for yourself starting with your feet and moving upward. One very effective visualization is seeing yourself as liquid light that can pour into any container and accept that pattern as its own.

Give yourself plenty of time to assimilate the changes as they take place. Shapeshifting cannot be rushed. You'll know you're succeeding when your awareness begins to change. You will take on new dimensions of sensation—in the way you perceive light, for instance, or aromas in the air. It will be like waking up to a whole new world in which the self is set aside momentarily, and the cloak of another person or thing covers your soul.

Once you've finished the transformation, follow your instincts. People who become animals often find themselves behaving like that animal. People who become stones might feel heavy, ancient, and very grounded.

Make a mental note of all the changes you feel, especially the sensory ones. What are you learning? What's the most important thing about this experience that you can take back into real life?

At some point, you will feel the energy of the shift wane. When it does, transform back by reversing the earlier process. *Do not*, under any circumstances, just *poof* back into yourself. This causes an incredible headache.

Relax, breathe deeply, and eat something like fresh vegetables to ground yourself in reality again.

Make notes of your experience and return to them when you try again. Look for the parts of your approach to shapeshifting that worked really well and concentrate on using these, making minor adjustments for the difference in model.

As with most things on the Adept's Path, you won't become a successful shapeshifter overnight. Don't get discouraged. Some people *never* learn it! The limitation here originates with an attachment to physical form and the strong right-brain thinking inherent in certain personalities. But part of advancing your magical proficiency also comes in recognizing when you don't have a talent for something.

An adept doesn't *have* to shapeshift or be a glamourist. In Witchcraft, the choice of tools and techniques is truly that: a choice. As long as adepts remain true to themselves, their spiritual vision, and the areas of proficiency they have developed, arts like these are simply icing on a cake already baked to near perfection.

CHAPTER FIVE

DREAMWORK

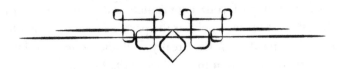

"Nothing so much convinces me of the boundlessness of the human mind as its operations in dreaming."
—William Benton Clulow

Recorded history shows the first written dream guides appearing in Egypt around 1300 BCE. From that time forward, dream interpretation and omen anthologies have surfaced in nearly every culture and era as a way for people to understand these strange night visitors. In the more detailed collections that remain for our scrutiny, the authors hypothesize that dreams indicate many things about the dreamer, including illness, fears, and desires. These books also indicate a strong belief that dreams act as harbingers, portents, and omens, and may even bear messages from the gods.

We know from modern psychological studies that it is far easier to receive messages from the subconscious while we sleep. It is also, therefore, easier to receive important information from the superconscious, the astral or spiritual plane, the universe, and the god/dess. Such information, once received, is very valuable for advancing our magical arts and assisting our quest for adeptness. since many of these things pass us by without notice during waking hours.

Everyone dreams, whether they remember it or not. So, what sets apart advanced magical dreaming from everyday pizza-generated dreams? Several things. First, the dreams discussed in this chapter will be those you generate through metaphysical methods. Second, the techniques used have distinctly magical goals and uniquely spiritual perspectives. Third, after dreaming, you will make an effort to recognize, integrate, and manifest the lessons or information in everyday life and all magical workings. Finally, on an even more advanced level, you will begin working magically with an entire group of like-minded dreamers.

THE DREAM DIARY

As unique insights from various sources filter down into our minds, it's important to have a record of them so integration can occur. Before going any farther into these methods, please find yourself a dream diary or a dependable tape recorder. Keep this next to your bed in a readily accessible spot. Immediately upon waking from a dream, write it down or record it in as much detail as possible. Include colors, sounds, smells, people, the way objects are placed (especially if unusual), conversations, animals, plants, and the like. As you do, note how much coverage each item got in the dream (was it central or cursory?).

When you feel you've written or talked yourself out, you can relax, go back to sleep, or wake up. If you do get up, give yourself a little time to let the fog of sleep clear before trying to interpret the dream's contents. Otherwise, you're liable to miss important nuances. Similarly, if you feel off that day, wait until another time to review the dream. Sickness, anger, frustration, and distraction can result in misinterpretations or worst-case-scenario perceptions, so it's really best to evaluate the symbols when you're centered and focused.

If you tend to remember your dreams during the day, you might want to keep a handheld tape recorder or spiral notebook with you in your briefcase, purse, or whatever so you can capture the information and look at it later. For evaluating the dream's contents in detail, I recommend a good dream guide *(Language of Dreams,* for instance; see the bibliography). Use the given symbolism and variants there as a measuring tool to which you add personal meaning and insights in healthy quantities. As you analyze the dream in detail, also bear in mind the following:

- The dream guide is only a sketchbook. The meaning something has for you should always be considered *first,* with all other possible interpretations examined afterward.
- Even when magically generated, not all dreams will have spiritual or religious meaning. Most, in fact, center on everyday issues that need addressing. Remember that no matter how adept you are magically, you are still human with human needs and problems. These internal and external factors can, and often do, evidence themselves when given a metaphysical doorway to walk through.
- Dream meanings don't have to be elusive. If your dream appears to have an obvious message or lesson, consider this first! You can still check the minute details for other symbolism but don't go crazy hunting for connotations that may not exist.
- Magical dreams manifest periodic instances of intense, three-dimensional precognition and post-cognition. Allow for such possibilities in your interpretations. Also, be prepared for the

physical and emotional effect this can have on you upon waking.
- Magical dreams can generate instances of astral projection to different places and times. These types of dreams are not common, but can be psychically, physically, and emotionally startling. Take care to rise slowly afterward to avoid a headache.
- Magical dreams may open the doorway to other planes of existence, including that of devas and human spirits. Consequently, conversations with deceased relatives or friends, or even fairy-folk, are a possibility. Don't automatically consider such visitations in dreams as symbolic rather than literal.
- What your dream means now and what it will mean three weeks from now can differ dramatically. Reread your dream diary regularly to gain additional insights based on what you know, what's happened recently, and what's going on presently.
- Numerous factors can influence your dreamtime, including noises, lights, odd smells in the environment, and the type of food you've eaten before bed. So, even if a dream occurred thanks to a magical nudge, it may turn out to be humorous or punny, or mean nothing whatsoever. Sometimes you may not even remember dreaming. Don't give up! As the old Buddhist saying goes, there are three keys to success: practice, practice, and practice.

THE SACRED SLEEP SPACE

Because magical dreaming opens psychic and spiritual doors within and without, it's prudent to consider setting up your dream space with some protective warding. Actually, most adept magical practitioners will tell you that creating a clean, safe region for any type of magic is a good idea. It not only keeps contrary forces out but also holds your power in place until the energy has been applied effectively.

In terms of protecting your sleep space and making it vibrationally suitable for a magical dream, you can turn to any personally preferred rituals or spells. If you don't have a specific one that you use, then try the following idea.

Burn incense blends that stress both protection (myrrh, patchouli, violet) and psychism (lilac, nutmeg, sandalwood) in a fire-safe container. Walk this around the bedroom clockwise three times to draw positive energy inward, then leave it near the bed. If you're attempting to banish a nightmare, walk counterclockwise.

Caution: Put the container at least an arm's length away. The smoke or aroma, if too intense, can disrupt sleep, and you don't want to run the risk of tipping over the container while sleeping.

Place charged symbolic objects as closely as possible to the four cardinal points of your room. Just before getting into bed, activate them by pointing to each one and using an invocation to the quarters. Here's one possible invocation to try:

> *"Guardians of the East, move into this space with the winds of Spirit. Carry me on gentle breezes to sleep that I may dream of you, and of magic, and be able to record the experience accurately."*

> *"Guardians of the South, move into this space with the spark of Spirit. Ignite in me warm, soulful fires that my sleep may be filled with you and magic yet wake with energy and power."*

*"Guardians of the West, move into this space with the
waves of Spirit. Wash me with inspired waters that
I may dream of you and of magic and understand
the message."*

*"Guardians of the North, move into this space with the
soil of Spirit. Root me in rich earth that while I dream
of you and magic, my spirit is safely home."*

Dismiss these guardians upon waking after you've written or recorded any dreams. Place some fish netting, to which you attach azurite, moonstone, or bits of silver, above the area where you sleep to encourage psychic or prophetic dreams. Make yourself a dream amulet using sand (representing the "sandman") as a base. To this, add some rosemary, lavender, mint, or thyme for peaceful sleep. Also, add marigold, rose, or bay to rouse the psychic self. Empower the mixture with an incantation like this:

*"Master of the Sands, bring me a magical dream, wrap
me in sleep beneath the Moon's beams."*

Keep this mix in a little bundle under your pillow or bed. If you don't mind vacuuming in the morning, sprinkle part of a mixture like this one on the floor around your bed. This creates a magic circle around you that will be further energized by invoking sacred space. (Probably best to avoid this method if you have pets, though!)

Bless and charge a sheet, pillow, blanket, or pajamas for safety and intuition while you sleep. Charging can be accomplished in several easy ways. One way is scenting the item with a sympathetic herbal sachet in the linen closet or drawer or washing it in aromatic water. Another way is leaving the item in the light of a full moon to accent both a fullness of protective power and the insight you hope to gain while dreaming. In either case, the result is that you are literally and figuratively wrapped in magic all night.

Pray, chant, tone, or play sacred music before going to sleep to invite protective, inspirational powers into the space to participate in your dreams.

Finally, as you feel yourself drifting off, visualize the entire room being painted in sparkling white-gold light (including all the ducts, windows, and so forth). Alternatively, envision yourself surrounded by a three-dimensional bubble of similarly protective light energy.

PERSONAL DREAMTIME MAGIC

The dream plane adds a dimension to magic that we often don't experience in waking hours: unconditional belief. Usually when we dream, we don't stop to consider the content's verity or the reality of the experience. And when miraculous things happen in dreams, like people flying, we don't question them either—they simply *are*. Combining this kind of trust with willpower and magical methodology creates amazing possibilities and a potent coalition that works together to manifest your goals.

People with sleep disorders or those who wake up at every little noise will discover another unique benefit to bedtime magic. Since you've created a sacred space before lying down (and often will be relaxed from meditation), it's more likely that you will sleep soundly. Sleeping soundly, in turn, allows your dream cycle to run its full course so that you can either finish the intended working or receive information and messages.

The sections that follow discuss some psychological approaches to dreaming mingled with magic, along with specifically metaphysical ones. Since dreams originate within the mind and magic is guided by willful thought, this blend should generate the best results. Please tinker with the procedures described until you find what works most effectively for you.

LUCID DREAMING

A lucid dream is one in which you realize you're dreaming and then interact with the dream to affect a positive outcome. For many people this proves difficult since it's uncommon to recognize a dream's occurrence until it's over. Nonetheless, on those occasions when you realize you're in the dream plane, seize the moment!

Most importantly, remember that your mind is the ruler of your dreams. What you think about happens. You need no words, only focused thought to manipulate the dream's progression (and the magical energy generated by that progression). It's wise, however, not to attempt to make changes too quickly, or you might lose the dream altogether.

Second, decide upon a definite metaphysical course to follow that makes sense in the dream's construct. For example, if you're dreaming of a forest stream flowing with clean, fresh water, one logical magical focus would be the Water element. Walk over to that stream, bathe in it to cleanse tension and maladies, drink of it to internalize inspiration, toss in a stone with a wish, or commune with the water devas who abide there. (Note: devic entities are not bound to the earthly plane, having both an earthly and an etheric presence.)

Don't think too hard or too long about what direction to take; this will disrupt the dream, and you may even wake up. Instead, allow your first instinct to guide you. Usually this impulse is right on the money with regard to what type of energy you most need to generate via the dream.

By the way, it is also possible to direct a dream from the perspective of a viewer instead of an active participant. Think of this like watching a movie whose actions you control: you're the director. Lucid dreaming using this positioning is particularly beneficial when you need a different outlook regarding the situation shown in the dream. If your mind is replaying difficulties from waking hours, then this is an alternative to consider. In this case, do still take control of the dream with your thoughts but stand back and watch yourself. Guide your interactions in the dream so they have a positive outcome that you can later apply in real time.

Once you've altered the dream and accomplished your spiritual or magical aim, allow the dream to run the remainder of its natural course (if you haven't already awakened). There may still be symbols or messages in this final portion that you can work with later. And as with all dreams, make notes of your experiences, especially how you feel after interacting with the dream. Ask yourself questions like:

- Did you feel the magical energy created during the dream, and if so, how was it different from that of waking spells and rituals?
- Did the magic of your dreamtime affect your waking mental perspectives or physical condition? If so, how?
- Were there unexpected events in the dream that may have had additional meaning to consider? Even in a lucid dream, especially one generated by metaphysical preparation, the universe may step in with some guidance or insights.
- Did interacting with the dream give you a greater feeling of control over your own mind, will, and the seemingly capricious whims of fate? If so, go with that feeling—it's part of the reward for your efforts.

- Finally, were you able to apply the lessons or visions in the dream to real life in a positive way? If so, how? This is very important. Whatever approach proves successful often generates lucid dreaming success again in the future.

PROGRAMMED DREAMING

The programmed dream varies slightly from the lucid dream. Now instead of interacting with a dream-in-progress, you pre-create a dream's progression or focus. This is accomplished by directing your attention to a specific symbol or suggestion just before going to sleep. Both approaches employ some type of meditation for the greatest success.

To try the symbolic approach, pick out an emblem that represents what you want to dream about or the magical energy you want to integrate. Runes make excellent emblems, as do many common magical sigils. For example, to receive an inspired healing dream or encourage healing energy, you might visualize the caduceus before going to sleep. To inspire a deeper understanding of the Goddess, you might visualize a full moon or a goblet (both of which are womb shaped). For insightful dreams, the Eye of Ra might work, and for magical knowledge, the pentagram is an excellent choice.

Any symbol that you can easily recognize and recall can become the focus in this methodology, including technological items and common modern logos. But in choosing a symbol for programmed dreaming, make sure that:

- The symbol is easily visualized in all its detail.
- The symbol adequately represents your needs or goals. If it doesn't feel quite right, keep looking until you find a representation that evokes a strong

spiritual and emotional response. Otherwise, this exercise will fall short.
- The symbol has personal meaning to you. For example, those following a Norse path might substitute the rune Kano for clear vision instead of the Eye of Ra because it's familiar in their spiritual tradition.
- The symbol's color harmonizes with your goal (note that you can change the hue in your visualization).

Next, look at the chosen symbol for a while before going to bed. Observe it from all angles and sides, put it in different types of lighting, and so on (this is especially helpful if the symbol is a three-dimensional object). Keep studying it until you can see the image as clearly in your mind with your eyes closed as when they're open.

Keep this image in mind as you begin breathing deeply, placing yourself into a relaxed semi-meditative state until you drift off. Make note upon waking of any dreams that come, especially if you feel they tie in with your chosen symbol. I suggest giving a symbol at least three tries before giving up on it. Sometimes it takes a while for the concept to filter into the subconscious strongly enough to elicit a related dream or manifest the related energy during waking hours.

To try the suggestion approach, pick out words or short phrases that represent the goal or energy you wish to create. In deciding what words or phrases you want to use, remember:

- Choose familiar words that you're comfortable with. This isn't the time for Shakespeare. Simplicity and meaning are the keys to success.
- Keep phrases brief. If they get too long, they won't have as strong an impact.

- Work in your native language, or one with which you are fluent. In some languages, minor errors in diction can change meanings dramatically.

After choosing words or phrases, tape-record them on a thirty-minute tape, repeating them softly over and over again. Some people find that playing music along with the words helps them relax and focus. If a tape recorder isn't handy, repeat the words or phrases to yourself (out loud or mentally) as you might a mantra until you fall asleep.

The repetition combined with meditation sets up a supportive environment for hypnotic or autosuggestion. The spoken words and phrases create vibrations in and around you to effect change. In user-friendly terms, think of it like an empowered affirmation that generates a dream or spiritual energy directed toward a goal while you sleep.

As a side note here, a personal mantra can become the key phrase for this exercise as long as you recognize that you cannot predetermine the effect this method will have on your dream's progression. A mantra consists of sacred sounds (like the *Om*) that vibrate on a special level, attuning the speaker to universal energy within and without. So, you might have a dream that deals with a pressing issue, a dream that includes missives from spirit guides, or even a vision rather than a programmed dream as I've defined the term. In either case, make notes of your experiences in your dream journal.

DIVINELY INSPIRED DREAMING

Ancient people turned to dreams looking for messages from the gods quite frequently. The Greeks, for example, felt dreams offered spiritual clarity. Certain Grecian oracles were said to use sacred sleeping as a method for divination.

Similarly, among the Hittites, Egyptians, and Japanese were specially ordained dreamers who isolated themselves in order to receive dreamtime messages from the gods.

Reviewing these historical accounts reveals several commonalities in the way people prepared for divine missives. Specifically, they would take a ritual bath, fast, and pray beforehand to cleanse the body and soul in order to make themselves acceptable to the Divine. Then the dreamer slept in a temple, promising to continue praying and sleeping there until the desired vision came.

Adapting these ideas isn't difficult, since many of the preparations are still common in magical practices. Take a ritual bath or shower to wash away tensions and purify your aura. Fast and meditate for a day beforehand as long as it's physically feasible. Before going to bed, a prayer might be combined with visualization or a mantra (see also Programmed Dreaming, page 103). But what about sleeping in a temple, historically called incubation?

These days, it would be hard to sleep in a church and not get arrested for vagrancy. Nonetheless, one of the goals of advanced Witchcraft and the Adept's Path is making your home into a sacred space. So, instead of sleeping in a temple, create a sacred sleeping space before asking for a dream from the God or Goddess. Also, don't forget that even without invoking the quarters or calling the Watchtowers, your body is a temple—the temple of your soul. As long as you treat it respectfully, this vessel accepts and integrates divine dreams perfectly well without any other aids being necessary (although they may prove helpful).

With all that said, the question becomes: How do you know if you've truly received a dream from the god/dess? We can begin answering this question by examining the accounts of the world's holy people for insight. In such accounts, the following signs indicated a divinely originated dream:

- The dream includes a bright, beautiful light that either precedes the information received or remains throughout the dream.
- The vision evokes strong emotional or physical responses (generated by the overwhelming power of the Sacred) that you can't easily verbalize. Words seem inadequate.
- The dream provides detailed information that you had no way of knowing. This is particularly true of prophetic dreams (see later in this section) or those that indicate a friend or family member in need of immediate aid. (Note: bear in mind that dreams of this last type can also be generated by telepathy or empathy.)
- A voice identifies itself as a specific deity in the dream (this is rare).
- The vision is accompanied by other sensory impressions that remain behind as clues to the god/dess who inspired the dream. For example, upon waking from a dream inspired by Apollo, the room might bear the lingering aroma of bay.
- Throughout the dream, no matter what you see, you have a feeling of comfort and welcome from a vast presence.
- The dream provides instructions on how to heal a personal malady or correct an injustice, or it offers other sound advice through easily recognizable—and very personal—imagery. Note, however, that such a dream can also come from spirit guides instead of the god/dess.

All in all, you are the only person who can qualify and quantify the dream experiences you have. Generally, however, anyone who truly receives a vision from the Sacred Parent will have few, if any, question about the source. Why? Because children instinctively recognize their parents, and because this parent is already part of your heart and soul.

PSYCHIC AND PROPHETIC DREAMING

In ancient times, people would travel from miles around to visit a dream oracle. Here, professional dreamers literally slept on the job, specifically to receive visions of the future. Since such centers were regarded as divinely inspired, these dreamers underwent the same types of rituals as those for receiving dreams from the gods—as can you, with one minor change. Many Witches believe that psychic and prophetic dreams may or may not be guided by a divine source. So, depending on your beliefs, you will be placing a request before Powers-that-be (or before your Higher Self) for a specifically psychic or prophetic dream. Burn lemongrass, lilac, nutmeg, or sandalwood to emphasize this request vibrationally.

No matter the source, these dreams augment magical goals and practices by opening insightful doorways that everyday life doesn't usually access. The psychic dream gives you an astral window, if you will. From this window you can observe a situation as if it were occurring in real time and so discover what is causing discomfort, develop solutions to problems, and glean other clarifying information to use in waking hours—with one important difference. As the dream unfolds, any number of psychic gifts begin manifesting themselves naturally, including telepathy, clairvoyance, and auric vision.

It doesn't particularly matter what psychic gift gets put into action during the dream state. What's most important is that this experience can result in a healthy nudge toward expressing such gifts while awake. This is especially true with individuals who are uncomfortable with their psychic aptitude or who haven't uncovered all of it yet.

Prophetic dreams cannot be wholly separated from psychic dreams since futuretelling is intimately connected with psychic insight. In this case, however, you move along the lines of time and dimension in astral form following the path of least resistance (which is also the direction in which energy flows naturally). Whether or not the vision is about something with which you're personally familiar is of no consequence—the key here is a knack for understanding fate's web and observing this progression from the dream state.

The difficult part is recognizing a prophecy when one comes. The dream timeline can move forward or back, and when this movement is slight (days or weeks), it's nearly impossible to detect a "futuristic" trend. This is why the dream diary is so important. It records hits and misses in your interpretations. As you reread your dream journal in the weeks and months ahead and discover prophetic trends, you will build the confidence necessary to begin trusting these images more.

Group Dreaming

Magic in the dreamtime takes on new dimensions, including the way in which we interact with other people who are also dreaming. In order to coordinate group dreaming successfully, every member of a group needs to follow certain procedures that are set in advance by the group or its leader. For example, it helps if everyone eats similar foods during the day and gets ample rest the night before attempting a group dream. It's also useful to have pre-agreed-upon preparations for everyone in ritually establishing the sacred sleep space. Other helpful guidelines include:

- Specify beforehand exactly what the group hopes to achieve by this effort (including central symbols, imagery, or other significant guideposts to watch for in the dream plane).
- Begin the pre-sleep ritual at the same time and end it at the same time (try using alarm clocks to help with this).
- Breathe deeply and rhythmically in a pattern known to all members. This helps bring the group spirit into harmony, even over distances.
- Burn the same types of incense. This is best prepared by the group in a ritual beforehand so each person can add their consonant energy to the blend.
- Wear ritual robes to bed, or other identifying items that are always with you during group work. These items are used to the group's energy and therefore help generate a singular mind.
- Prepare a guided meditation on tape that everyone can listen to as they fall asleep. This is best created by the group's leader, or whoever generally guides the group through visualizations. Note that this tape should include key symbols or phrases that reflect the group's goal.

There are several reasons that groups try dreaming as a unit, but the primary reasons are group coherence and harmony. We shed a lot of facades and unnecessary attitudes during sleep because there's no one else around to impress or put off. Consequently, a successful group dream meeting can result in a profound deepening of the group's awareness of its members as they truly are, without pomp and circumstance.

A second reason is to tend to someone who is far away from the group. In the astral, there is nothing to hinder the way we touch people, no matter where they may be. In this case, preparations can be made in advance for the person in need to join the group in the dream plane and receive assistance. Make sure, however, to take into account any changes in time zone so that everyone's working concurrently.

A third reason is to meet in the group's astral temple and cast spells, perform a ritual, or gather knowledge. Working in an astral temple relieves some of our attachment to worldly things, as does the dreaming itself, so integration of any gathered knowledge improves. In this setting, it is also much easier to generate and guide the magic—the astral realm is magic's natural habitat.

After following the group's dreaming procedure, all members should get up and record their experience (even if they don't remember anything). Note the time you woke up, your very first impression of how you feel and what happened, and then any other details you can recall. Take this dream diary with you to the next group meeting so you can compare notes and gauge the attempt's success.

All in all, the greatest advantage to spiritually centered dreaming is putting otherwise unproductive hours to work for important, fulfilling goals. With life's hectic pace, whatever time we can find to honor the Sacred and empower our magic is very precious. In sleep, most of us have six to eight hours a day to give to this goal and continue our path toward mastery.

CHAPTER SIX
TRANCEWORK AND PATHWORKING

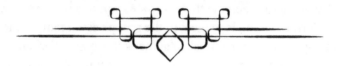

"Two roads diverged in a wood, and I—I took the one less traveled by, and that has made all the difference."
—Robert Frost

I have chosen to discuss these two methods in the same chapter because they are intimately associated. It is all but impossible to experience an effective pathworking exercise if you do not know how to enter a deep trance state. Similarly, the focus and resolve necessary for pathworking will significantly improve any trance efforts.

The interrelatedness of pathworking and trancework is a natural component for many spiritual pursuits. This connection, which is part of a magical web, entangles all metaphysical methodology. Some ancient and modern magi choose to master one school or method (like glamoury or necromancy). Even so, most recognize the value of becoming proficient in several alternative or complementary techniques, recommending this diversification to their students as well.

Then each student can continue along the path toward adepthood by gaining the necessary knowledge and skills that round out all magical endeavors.

TRANCE WORK

"And all my days are trances, and all my nightly dreams..."
—Edgar Allan Poe

The word *trance* has several origins. In French, it means "an apprehensiveness caused by approaching evil." In Spanish, the word translates as "the hour of death," and in Latin, it means "a passage"—something you go beyond or across. All three of these definitions speak to our research into advanced trance working. Specifically, they reveal that the trance state transcends normal perceptions and takes us to a new type of knowing, similar to that which a soul experiences upon release from the Earth plane.

In simpler terms, trance is a state of the soul wherein it exists outside of normal time, space, and dimensions. From this new, temporary plane of existence, we can see and sense things that would be very difficult to experience in the confines of physical form. Trance mimics a dreamlike condition that expands our consciousness into alternative dimensions of reality, deepens magical comprehension, broadens our awareness of emotions, and releases the spiritual self.

The trance begins with deep, quiet meditation (sometimes combined with visualization) that encourages complete relaxation and directs mental energy away from temporal thought processes. Any meditation technique you presently use can help you obtain a trance state but now you'll take your efforts one step further. Start by using slow, rhythmic breathing to loosen your muscles and liberate your mind.

Continue breathing in a metered, all-connected manner until you reach the point where your body experiences sensations similar to those just before sleep. Some people describe this as a mental and physical buzz in which the body feels very heavy and connected to Earth by its gravity, while others say there's no awareness of the physical whatsoever. In either case, feel yourself detaching from the temporal and leaving it behind.

Let your spirit begin to break free and float across the veil between worlds. In your mind's eye, you may envision this veil appearing like a sheet of effervescent light-fabric or a bridge of illuminated particles. Once across this barrier, your spirit can work magic or pursue spiritual goals unhindered by the body's normal limitations.

What goals are suited to trance states? Actually, far more than you might immediately imagine. You can accomplish much when focused wholly on Spirit, including approaching spirits or guides for important information, seeking out spiritual visions for personal growth and transformation, communing with spirits or channeling them, and ecstatic divination. I will discuss all of these intentions in more depth later in this chapter.

Trance Partners

Because our minds in a trance interact freely with Spirit to interpret the experience, we often perceive the astral landscape as similar to reality. Let go and follow the imagery before you but make note of specific landmarks along the way. Use these landmarks (like the veil) as guides for safely entering and leaving the trance state. This alertness is important because the astral world feels very natural and comfortable to our spirits. Without such guideposts, we can wander around to the point of losing ourselves.

Given such possibilities, I recommend finding a partner who will watch over you during deep trancework, at least when you first begin trying it. Think of this partner as akin to a set of training wheels on a new bike: someone who'll keep you safe and help you find your way home if you accidentally get lost or distracted in the astral reality.

The job of an astral partner is simply observation. They check your breathing throughout the trance and watch for any signs of distress. While most people have positive experiences on the astral, some not-so-pleasant entities and energies exist there, too. If your spiritual second notices you grimacing, crying out, flailing, or doing anything else that indicates you've encountered an unproductive situation, they will slowly help bring you back to self through guided visualization and physical touch, the latter of which provides grounding and a reconnection to the Earth plane. Consequently, it's important that your watcher knows you somewhat intimately as this will help them gauge what they observe more accurately.

Similarly, if you don't return for a long time (I don't suggest staying in a trance for much more than an hour), your partner might decide to do a spot check. Here, they speak in very soft tones to ask you for a specific sign that all is well (like squeezing a hand). Their voice will come to you like a song or echo from far away and let you know that you've been away quite a while. The spot check is very important because, just like the astral landscape, the timeline during trances can be very deceptive. Hours might seem like minutes, or vice versa.

If your watcher feels that you're lost or confused, they may choose to come into your experience and guide you back. This is accomplished by placing themselves in a *light* meditative state while holding a pulse point in their strong hand. Slowly, they will attune their breath to yours and pour out spiritual energy in your direction. This energy is like a lifeline that floats to wherever you've traveled, offering aid. It may appear like a snake, a thin wave, a streak of light, a twig, an arm, or another item that has a similar shape. When it comes, you can either grab hold and follow it back home or turn it around so it returns to the watcher who will then know that all is well.

When your journey is over, the watcher should have water and some grounding foods like raw vegetables ready for you. Allow them to serve you during this adjustment time (you will provide the same service to them at a later date). Move slowly, reconcile yourself to the experience, and make notes of it. Then, when you're fully back to self, discuss the trance with your partner. Ask them for their impressions so you can include them in your journal entry.

Note: I do not suggest becoming the watcher for someone on the same day you've attempted or achieved a trance state yourself. These techniques take a lot of concentration and personal stamina, and you won't be as alert as you should be for such an important task. I also don't recommend trying to achieve more than one trance a day. You'll usually find the second attempt far less productive due to diminished energy.

Most practitioners find that partnering is very beneficial for both people. Each gets to observe from within and without the transformations that take place during a deep trance state. Upon returning, each has the chance to bounce ideas off the other for insight and an alternative perspective on the experience.

GROUP TRANCES

Achieving a group trance state is very difficult. It takes a leader who is highly sensitive to interpersonal dynamics as well as each participant's meditation pace. While groups that have worked together for a long time experience some level of success in using prerecorded meditations for group trancing, I personally feel having a trance guide is more effective and safer. The leader (who is the "guide" for the whole group) can then also act as the watcher, making sure everyone stays together and focused.

The primary purpose for group trance work is to solidify a group's identity and find a common ground from which to work during real time. One common approach is to have the leader direct a deep meditation and breathing exercise. Unified breath brings the individuals assembled into synergy with one another. Once this synergy is achieved, the leader then might direct each member to visualize their spirit as a light form within a huge energy bubble. Here, the individual spirit lights shift and merge into oneness, a harmonious diversity.

From the power bubble, the group can direct magic for collective creation if they choose—but this is not the main focus of the exercise. Instead, the nucleus of attention is observing the way each person's energy interacts with that of other group members, for both good and ill. Careful scrutiny by the leader during this time will prove very helpful in all group interactions to follow. Mental observation by the participants will help them in working cooperatively with one another, too. Within the trance sphere, people perceive one another in total truth.

As a side note, this visualization is common, but it's by no means the only one used. Leaders often change imagery to suit different goals. For example, they might direct the spirit lights into a circle of trees for an astral ritual, or into a pool of light for group caregiving.

When leaders feel the energy or attention in the room waning, they will reverse whatever process they used in generating the trance and bring everyone back to normal awareness. It's important that this step isn't rushed and that the group's members remain quiet while other people adjust. Part of group trancing is teaching the participants to be sensitive to each other's working tempo, which then becomes a foundation for all future magic.

I should note at this point that during a group effort, people often discover feelings about (and for) members of which they weren't consciously aware. Be prepared for post-trance expressions of misgivings, love, passion, and other strong emotions. This post-trance time of integration and expression is very important and should be encouraged even among people who don't normally speak up. By so doing, the group can begin cleaning out residual negativity and accepting people just as they are. It's also a time when folks can offer support and understanding for difficult rectifications. Try to guide these sessions sensitively, encouraging constructive communication followed by positive action.

INFORMATION RETRIEVAL FROM SPIRIT

In many shamanic traditions, shamans use the trance state as a means of approaching the spirit world and asking for information (see also Chapter Seven). For example, they might ask a disease spirit what the cause of sickness is and what offerings or magical aids will banish the problem. The reason for choosing this methodology varies by individual. In cases where you are calling upon a human spirit, it's safer than calling it into yourself (mediumship) or summoning it into the temporal world (necromancy). In instances where other types of spirits are sought, the trance state opens the pathway for effective communication.

Certain commonalities appear in trances designed specifically for gaining knowledge. For example, many seekers abstain from sexual interaction or food for a certain number of days beforehand to purify themselves and focus wholly on Spirit. This clears away a lot of mundane clutter that can either disrupt information retrieval or cloud it.

To move into the ecstatic trance state, you might chant, dance, drum, pray, provide offerings, pour out libations, don a mask (to honor the spirit sought), or enter into darkness (like a cave). This last approach encourages sensory deprivation so that you leave the material world completely behind. Additionally, emerging from the darkness is like a rebirth or renewal.

If you intend to use a trance to gain knowledge, any or all of these methods are perfectly valid. But before jumping in with both feet, take the following steps:

- Decide if you want a trance partner, and if so inform them fully about your plans.
- Have a specific goal in mind. What exactly are you trying to learn?
- Determine a specific spirit whose insight you want to seek. This is the only spirit that should approach you. If any others come into the astral tapestry, you have every right to send them away.
- Set up a protected sacred space for your work.

The spirit sought in this exercise can be that of a god or goddess, a guide, an animal, a plant, or even a mineral whose metaphysical or symbolic attributes would be useful in answering a question. For example, you might seek out a chameleon spirit for insights on how to blend into uncomfortable surroundings or call upon a tree spirit to teach you how to root yourself and seek out spiritual water.

These two examples also reveal that trance states offer an excellent vehicle for shapeshifting. Here you still commune with a spirit but take the activity a little farther by altering your aura to mirror this spirit. In so doing, you accept the spirit's predominant characteristics and outlooks, activating these attributes in your auric field. You can then use the associated skills and perspectives in answering the question at hand (see also Chapter Four).

Don't try to anticipate what type of answers or insights you'll receive. Some people get literal replies while others get symbolic or sensory ones. For example, you might hear words, get empathic replies, see a significant emblem, feel a textural quality in your hands, or smell a meaningful aroma. Make a mental note of these cues but don't let them interrupt the trance. More information may still be forthcoming.

At some point during the experience, the spirit you've called upon will withdraw, the energy wane, and the astral tapestry start to fade. This means you've accomplished all you can during the session. Slowly adjust your breathing to its normal pace. Doing so naturally calibrates your awareness to consciousness. After you've relaxed for about fifteen minutes, make notes of the experience and return to it later to meditate upon the meaning. A deep trance for information retrieval takes a lot of personal energy and may leave you feeling a little fuzzy around the edges. You'll find that your ability to interpret the trance experience improves with rest and emotional space.

CHANNELING

As you've seen, some trances give you access to various entities or a closer union with the Sacred. At any point during the communion, you can choose to move aside momentarily, allowing the entity or sacred power to flow through you. The purpose here is one of imparting information directly instead of waiting until after the trance is over to interpret things (see also Chapter Three, and Chapter Seven).

Trance channeling has many forms. In the Craft, you'll rarely see the flamboyant public displays that came under close scrutiny during the early 1990s. Instead, channeling trances are often used to direct energy from Spirit for a specific goal like healing, divination, or getting an answer to a pressing question through automatic writing. In the trance state, the adept's spirit is able to step aside and let greater powers do the work. When done correctly, the results are nearly miraculous, because the human factor has to some degree been filtered out.

Here is a list of recommended preparations for trance channeling:

- Try to drink a fair amount of water that day to cleanse your body but stop several hours before your meditation so your efforts aren't interrupted by nature's call.
- Get a good amount of rest in the days preceding the attempt. Trance channeling requires a lot of personal control and focus.
- Consider having a trance partner who can not only monitor you but also record the experience. If not, have an audio recorder set up to catch any important missives that you might not recall upon returning to normal awareness.

Once you achieve the trance state, remember that your spirit and body have an intimate relationship. If a spirit or higher power wishes to use your body, it needs to ask permission, and you always have the right to say no. Similarly, if you find a field of coursing energy in the astral, you are the final determinant as to whether or not to allow this energy to flow through you to help manifest a goal. Carefully appraise what you see, hear, feel, and sense to determine if this energy source or spirit is a good one for the task or goal at hand.

More information about working with spirits will be covered in the next chapter under "Mediumship."

PROPHETIC TRANCES

The trance state can open up numerous psychic functions, including that of prophecy. Like the ancient seeress in some early Germanic and Norse cultures known as the Völva, you may enter a trance specifically to look into the future. As with the Völva, this is not a jaunt to appease simple curiosity. It is undertaken when pressing matters and a lack of perspective plague you or someone who has come to you seeking aid.

By relaxing and releasing yourself to the trance, you can often throw off the muddled outlooks that come from physicality and daily tensions and thereby gain a clearer understanding of what's up. Taking this one step farther, an adept who knows what signs to watch for in the astral landscape during a trance can discern those that indicate a timeline.

As with all astral landscapes, the way a timeline looks to adepts varies with the way they interpret the imagery. In some instances, it appears as a fiber or strand in a tapestry; in other cases, it's a road or path; in others still, it can look like a window on the horizon. No matter the imagery, however, adept seers can follow the portrait's metered progression to one possible future. Since humans tend toward ritualistic and habitual behavior, the resulting prophecy often proves at least partially correct.

To prepare yourself for this kind of effort, follow all the same steps as those for channeling or communing with the Divine. Knowledge of the future isn't hidden, but it is often safeguarded from those who would misuse it. Physical, spiritual, and mental preparation help overcome these safeguards. More important, this groundwork helps when it comes to detaching yourself from personal opinions as to what you *think* the future holds. An adept or elder is not immune to bias or preconceptions. Such bias can taint the way you perceive the astral landscape and its signs, thereby also tainting your interpretation. In order to act responsibly toward your psychic gifts, you need to maintain as pure an outlook as possible.

Since prophecy is a kind of information retrieval, keep a symbol (or a phrase) of your goal in mind all the while you work. It's important to find the right timeline, and the right window into the future.

You can't accomplish this if your mind is filled with other matters. Once you do find a timeline to follow, make mental notes of everything seen along the way. These are not only guideposts to follow back but also may add symbolic value to the interpretation later. Note that guideposts don't have to be visual—sounds and smells fit into this category, too.

At some point in the trance, you will realize that you can go no further. A brick wall might appear, you might start feeling very weary, or your vision might blur. This means that you have seen as much of the future landscape as you can for now, or that fate's web is too tangled to get more information. At this juncture, return along the path you followed and reestablish normal waking awareness.

Make a note of all the imagery you saw. Share this with the querist without trying to make any interpretations at first. This gives them an opportunity to figure out the meaning on an intuitive level for themself. Afterward, you can talk about the experience and point out symbolic dimensions that they may not have recognized or for which they had no frame of reference. Remind the querist, however, that the future isn't carved in stone. We always have free will. Every thought and action they have from this point forward can alter their future path.

If this trance was done solely for personal information, then I suggest taking a break before digging too deeply into an interpretation. While some prophetic trances will be quite literal, a fair majority are symbolic (symbols being the universe's form of shorthand). This shorthand notation may take a while to decipher, and it's much more easily accomplished after some rest and recuperation.

PATHWORKING

In simplest terms, pathworking entails intense, vivid meditation and visualization that take place in the trance state. Pathworking usually takes a longer time to accomplish than normal meditations or visualizations and actually represents the next natural step for both these methods. In some instances of intense path working, the guide for the effort will recommend a preparation period. During this time, you'll undertake various prescribed exercises, each of which has a theme and focus similar to the path working effort. This builds a strong foundation for a successful attempt.

Each pathworking effort has a distinct goal and imagery that draws you along the road toward that goal. Unlike guided meditation, however, you as the listener are not uninvolved in the way this exercise unfolds. As the exercise evolves, you'll be encouraged to ask questions, listen to a voice or sound, make choices, or answer a challenge. The resulting question, answer, action, or decision is considered inspired by a Divine or cosmic consciousness and therefore defines the rest of the path followed and how it affects you. This means that your pathworking guide must be very sensitive to your reactions so they can heed Spirit's leading and change the exercise accordingly.

One of the best examples of this is the Fenris (the wolf spirit of Teutonic mythology) pathworking that I've experienced in several different settings. Here, the pathwork's goal is getting in touch with, and releasing, the instinctive person within, specifically the wolf spirit that represents all that is wild and free. You as the pathworker listen to the voice of the animal within and are asked if you wish to follow it. If you choose to accept this part of yourself, attune to it, and then become one with it, the pathworking landscape continues.

This particular pathworking exercise allows you to choose the animal that you become (rather than a wolf)—one that symbolizes you more accurately. At this juncture, the pathwork takes on many of the attributes of a shapeshifting exercise, except that questions or choices are directed to the animal being. In either case, the goal is to better understand a different aspect of self, one more intimately connected with the natural world.

In order for a pathworking exercise to be really potent and meaningful, it's best led by someone who's already adept at guided visualizations. Audio recordings cannot respond to the way an individual interacts with the pathworking, and they don't allow for guidance from Spirit, so I really don't suggest a recorded effort. On the other hand, there's nothing that says you can't participate in designing a pathworking effort for yourself. In fact, this is often much more productive. Familiarity encourages relaxation, which in turn improves the trance state.

In designing pathworking efforts, the following guidelines may prove helpful:

- Determine the goal of the pathworking.
- Determine the astral landscape most suited to this goal. If you're having trouble, you might just be looking too hard. Natural settings are best for working with spirit animals, for example, while manufactured settings are suited to more mundane considerations. Remember, pathworking can be designed to assist with any spiritual, physical, mental, or mundane goal, including helping you function better on the job, improving your relationships, and the like.
- Consider elemental and symbolic correspondences as helpmates in designing the astral landscape. For example, water imagery is excellent for pathworking that deals with emotional issues. Water improves emotional "flow" and can also heal emotional wounds. A circle of fire is good for dealing with anger or passion.

Note: some guides choose not to predetermine the landscape but allow pathworkers to describe what they find and then work within this imagery. This approach requires a very creative and sensitive guide who can easily adapt the process to nearly any scenario.

With your goal in mind, ask yourself: what question(s) or choices should be posed in the pathworking? What obstacle(s), if any, should stand between you and the goal? For example, in ancient stories, the knight was always challenged with a question or riddle to determine if his intentions were pure.

Once you achieve a deep trance state, the query posed need not be complicated. In fact, simple questions seem to work best: what is your quest? Why have you come here? This type of question clarifies and solidifies your intention in your own heart. It also redirects your focus away from achieving the trance state to the work at hand.

What signs or symbols will act as beacons so that both you and your guide know when an exercise is coming to fruition? Some guides, for example, use an astral door that the pathworker steps through initially. When the pathworker finds another door, this indicates either a choice to alter the path or possibly end it.

As you can see, there are a lot of variables in creating pathworking exercises, and the variables can often change during the exercise. This means that both the pathworker and the guide need to be prepared for nearly every eventuality. You don't want minor changes to disrupt the constructive atmosphere of the exercise through distraction or abruptly bring a pathworker out of a trance. If either occurs, stop and try again another day.

Below, you will find two pathworking examples described from the perspective of the pathworking guide. These illustrations are subject to change depending on who uses them. Once you enter the astral landscape, you have the will and the means to alter its course, especially if guided by Spirit to do so. Consider these examples as rough formats. Change them by adding color, texture, personalized symbols, and flavors better suited to the objective at hand and the pathworker's leadings during the exercise.

The Self-Mirror

This exercise is intended to help us see ourselves as we truly are, in heart and soul.

Preparations: If possible, time this ritual for the dark moon, so that the pathworker can see the self in honesty without emotions and baggage from the past tainting that image. The dark moon acts as a substitute for performing the ritual in a cave.

Alternatively, work at dawn when the light of logic and reason mingles with the darkness of instinct and insight. Prior to this, the pathworker should bathe in purifying herbs, allowing all preconceptions to wane as the water washes them away. They should abstain minimally from meat for three days, and fast for a day, if possible.

Have the pathworker sit down and begin meditating alone. As you notice their tension wane and their breathing take on a slow, even pace, help them go into a deeper trance. This can often be accomplished by counting slowly backward and verbalizing suggestions about changes in her awareness.

One method that I use goes like this:

"Ten: You feel yourself relaxing even more, the tensions and thoughts of the day are flowing away from you and leaving behind peace.

Nine…eight…seven: You are physically sleepy but spiritually awake. You feel something happening on the edge of your awareness.

Six…five…four: Your body seems all but gone now. You are aware of your breath and heartbeat but all else has faded.

Three…two…one: You have arrived. This is a place outside of time and space where anything is possible. Welcome."

At this juncture, you begin the pathworking exercise.

The Path

Guide speaks to the pathworker, saying: *"See yourself in a wooded grove by night. Overhead the stars twinkle as if pleased to have company. Around you, Earth is alive and vibrant with sound. The crickets and an owl welcome you in song. Look all around you. Can you see a path or an opening?"* (Wait until the pathworker indicates they have found one.)

"Follow the path. It leads into deep darkness. Slowly, the trees seem to fade. The crickets and owls grow silent. The stars are gone. All that surrounds you is darkness, the sound of your breath, and the beating of your heart. Can you hear these?" (Wait for affirmation.)

"You know there is more here than the darkness. You can feel something on the edge of your awareness. Do you choose to try to find what awaits you here?" (Wait for affirmation.)

"Reach your hands out into the darkness. Find anything to cling to.

Follow a wall or vines, follow the stone beneath your feet… follow the leading of your heart's beating. It echoes in this place, and you can follow that sound…deeper and deeper still until you hear water just before you.

As you approach the water, a faint glow illuminates the area, and you see you are in a cave. In front, there lies a river and a raft with someone steering the helm. The figure is hooded, their face dark and stern. He turns to you, asking: Would you cross the river? Would you dare to see the truth?" (Wait for the pathworker to respond.) *"And what token will you give me for safe passage?"* (Wait again. It may take the pathworker some time to come up with an idea of what they can give, and it's okay to give a gentle nudge with this. For example, suggest they check in a pocket to see if anything appropriate is there.)

"The figure seems pleased by your thoughtful token and beckons for you to get on the raft. Do you climb on?" (Wait.) *"The waters of the river seem to move swiftly below you, yet the raft is steady and firm—just as firm as your spiritual quest. It lands safely on the other side. The figure tells you he will wait until your task is done and bring you back, then points toward an opening in the cavern wall above."*

"Where do you go?" (Wait—the assumption here is that the pathworker will follow the figure's leading.) *"The climb is difficult. Stones fall beneath your feet, and handholds sometimes give way, yet your resolve and strength are sure. Keep climbing until you reach that opening, then step in and rest for a moment."* (Pause here to let the pathworker assimilate the changing scenes.)

"Inside the opening, the walls are studded with small crystals and gems. Each seems to glow from within and sing a song all its own. None strives to be like another, yet all exist in harmony. These stones are your life's experiences; they blend together to create you. Follow the light they provide to the back of this opening." (Wait until you sense the pathworker has reached this spot.)

"On the wall here, you can see a round metal object. Grab hold of it and command it, saying, 'Mirror, mirror, reveal to me who I am and what I'll be.' Turn the mirror around and look upon its surface. Slowly an image will emerge that will show you all that you are, and all that you can become." (Note: give the pathworker about ten minutes here unless they seem done before this. It's important that she has time to see the full imagery that the mirror provides.)

"When you are done, return to the ferryman so he can bring you safely across the astral waters back home. When you land on that shore, your breathing begins to return to normal. When you feel ready, open your eyes." (After this point, a discussion can ensue about the experience. The pathworker does not have to share what they saw in the mirror if they don't wish to; it can be very personal.)

The Fairy Path

Note: Consider using this ritual again in Chapter Seven when wishing to commune with devic powers.

Preparations: If possible, time the path working for a time of year known for its fairy activity. Beltane (May Day), Lammas, and Samhain are all good possibilities. Alternatively, time the effort for a full moon to illuminate and augment the intuitive self.

Fill the room with natural aromas from incense, potted plants, fresh water, some rich soil, leaves, and the like. These aromas shouldn't be overwhelming, just enough to tease and awaken the pathworker's senses. Place several candles on the floor in front of them so they look like a road leading away from the pathworker.

At this point, proceed with the countdown described in the previous exercise or another pre-agreed-upon technique for deepening the trance state. When you feel the pathworker is ready, begin.

The Path

(Guide speaks to the pathworker, saying): *"Seeker, there is a path before you. Slowly open your eyes and see the light marking your way. Look upon the path until you can see it clearly in your mind's eye and then close your eyes once more."* (Wait for the pathworker to close their eyes.) *"Now, see yourself on this pathway. It reaches forward slowly, turning into a bright green line of grass in a meadow surrounded by ancient oaks."*

"At the boundary of the path and the meadow there stands a guardian holding a staff. The guardian stops you, placing the staff across the path.

The guardian turns, looking stern and curious, and asks: 'Do you wish to enter the meadow and follow the path further?'" (Wait for a response.)

"The guardian still doesn't move but stares at you with a look that pierces your very soul. She asks: 'Why have you come to the sacred grove?'" (Wait again for a response.) *"She moves aside, looking content, and says: 'Then enter and may your quest be fulfilled. Know, however, that the fairies have a will and ways all their own. You cannot command them, nor coerce their friendship. Walk the path, sit down, and let them find you.'*

As you turn to thank the guardian for letting you pass, you notice the entire landscape is now nothing but forest and glade. The guardian disappears into a cloud of stars that seem to spark and dance playfully as she goes. Listen to the sound they make. Can you hear them singing? What are the words of this ancient song?" (Pause to let the pathworker integrate any messages at this point.)

"When the sparks join the sky, move on. Look down and follow the bright grass path to a huge old tree. Walk quietly... reverently. This is sacred fairy land. Sit down beneath the tree. Extend some type of greeting to the fey; tell them why you've come." (Pause, watching for signs that the pathworker has completed this task.)

"Now wait and watch. Do not expect the fairy-folk to look like those in a book. They are grand and beautiful, filled with the power of Earth and the cosmos. They sparkle with dewdrops and starlight. They abide in raindrops, trees, sunlight, and the song

of the wind. Welcome them to you. Listen well to their words, and nod to me when they've gone."

(Pause for five to ten minutes here, waiting for the pathworker's nod. Fairies can be long-winded. Then take them out of the sacred grove, along the pathway of candles, back to normal awareness. At this point, you can discuss the experience with them to help with integration and retention.)

GROUP PATHWORKING

Since pathworking is very intimate, it is difficult to accomplish much in a group setting; I really don't recommend it except in groups that have worked magic together successfully for some time. The more people you have, the more variations on the theme there become. Unless you have a very harmonious group mind, then, group pathworking is tricky at best.

If you choose to attempt a group pathworking, start small—no more than three people—and see how it goes. If this works well, then slowly add more participants, carefully chosen, into future attempts. Make note of the types of pathworking efforts that seem most effective with your group (and with specific combinations of individuals within that group). Share these insights with other groups looking for good prototypes. Here's one example:

The Group Astral Temple

The group astral temple is created as a semi-permanent structure in the astral landscape. Here, the group can meet for dreamworking, trancework, or any other types of magic they choose within a protected, sacred space.

Preparations: Everyone finds a comfortable position—*not* lying down, in most instances. Unless everyone is very proficient, you will shortly hear snoring instead of traveling going on! You can take off your shoes or loosen clothing a bit so you don't feel constricted. If your group wants to do this together, someone can prerecord the path working, or one person can volunteer to lead the exercise.

The Path

"See a door in all its detail. Open the door. It leads to a dark passage. Follow the passage to a set of stairs moving downward. Notice that it's very dark. You can only see one stair ahead of where you are standing at all times. Don't let this deter you. Continue to descend and relax." (Pause so everyone gets to the bottom of the stairs.)

"When you reach the bottom, it is comfortably warm, the perfect temperature, as if the space is welcoming you. It is now that you realize you are actually within yourself, within your private sacred space in the temple of your heart. You are standing in the center of your circle in your sacred space. You walk to the East, then South, then West, then North, acknowledging each element and energy while redefining your sacred circle." (Pause.)

"You complete the circle and return to the East; when you are finished, you turn toward the center of the circle. Here, you find a narrow stairway without railings. It winds straight up into darkness, and the staircase is only wide enough for one person to walk. You can choose not to climb it, but it calls to you.

As you begin climbing, your feet are very unsteady. Concentrate on your balance; keep your eyes focused on your feet. The steps are each made of stone covered with moss and sand. The worn cracks show that they are ancient beyond human invention. You continue to rise one step at a time, feeling each little imperfection on each step in the soles of your bare feet." (Pause.)

"One step at a time—right, then left, then right, then left, with your arms raised slightly from your sides—you begin to

find your balance and become comfortable on the stairs. You raise your eyes slowly, one step at a time, and let your feet find their way alone with confidence.

The steps become smoother as you rise through the darkness, darkness that seems to be alive with a light just beyond your mind's reach. Up you go, right, then left, then right, then left." (Track the steps with your hands to keep the pace, slowly tapping out right and left.) *"Around you bright points of light ignite in the darkness, and you continue to rise toward them, looking ever upward at the staircase which disappears above you."* (Pause.)

"Without glancing down, you realize that the stairs have become completely smooth and feel almost liquid to the touch of your feet. A faint radiance seems to be coming from beneath your feet and you know this comes from the stairs, which have become translucent and appear to be made of sparkling glass. You realize now that the points of light are stars. The radiance here surrounds you in all directions as far as the eye can see. The galaxies are visible as massive swirling motes of light shot through with colors of every hue.

You continue to rise, comfortable and balanced upon the staircase on which you have now traveled for such a vast distance. You realize that the staircase is no longer visible before you and that, while you still feel it beneath your feet, it seems to have disappeared. Around you everything begins to take on a grayness. A sense of vastness and timelessness overwhelms you as you continue to rise." (Pause.)

"Everything now is gray; no stars and no galaxies swirl about you.

You realize that you have reached the top of the staircase and entered the astral plane. Here, you stop and stand still in the endless silence; you are a part of this vast gray silence, a consciousness that can exist here comfortably. You turn while standing in place, one full revolution all around. As you do, a short but wide avenue begins to take shape. You see every detail of the paving, and each leaf of the trees that march in straight rows down either side of the avenue. At the very end of this road, you see a massive temple, sitting proudly." (Pause.)

"Walk toward the temple, feeling the ground beneath your feet, and sensing the dappling of light as it passes through the leaves overhead. Continue down the path, taking note of the temple's pyramidal shape. It appears to be constructed of a solid crystal, semi-precious stone. It has one doorway, which stands directly before you. The door is without handle or knob, and has no keyhole, being made of the same material as the temple itself. Do you have the key to this door?" (Pause.) *"Look in your pockets, in your hand, around the stairs nearby!*

Somewhere, a sacred object, a talisman, the key to your astral being exists nearby or with you. When you find it, turn this item over in your hand and learn each of its characteristics. Feel its texture and temperature. Raise your eyes and look at the door again. Realize that there is a slight depression in its center that is the exact size and shape of your talisman.

Place your talisman here. The door swings wide open. Step into the temple and catch your breath. The scene before you is magnificent. Contained within is an endless, lovely garden. Trees and flowers grow in varieties never before imagined. The air is the perfect temperature for you, and there is just the slightest of breezes, carrying the sweet scent of blossoms." (Pause.)

"Slowly step forward. As you do, you'll hear the babbling of a stream that flows through the garden from somewhere off on your right and ends in a small pool on your left. Above, the trees portray each season. One is covered with blossoms drifting down quietly upon the breeze, another is heavily laden with fruit, still more are covered in autumn leaves or totally barren. No matter the greenery, all blossom in stars." (Pause.)

"Continue walking slowly about the garden. Find a meandering path and enjoy walking it. You can hear the animal

inhabitants of this garden rustling in the underbrush; there are birds singing from somewhere as well. Stand quietly and let these inhabitants introduce themselves." (Pause.) "*Introduce yourself to them.*

Now you notice another small path, or one of the animal inhabitants runs off in a particular direction. Follow it. In a very short time, you will come to a secluded location, surrounded on all sides by heavy growth. The path ends here. This glade abounds with an incredible feeling of peace and serenity." (Pause.)

"*At the back of the glade, you notice a small rock outcropping and see a spring of purest water bubbling up from the ground. This is the source of the stream and the source of wisdom. If you stand here and listen carefully, the fountain's sound will begin to resemble speech. Pay close attention to this message. It will be important for personal or group use.*" (Remember to discuss this message after the exercise.)

"*Now turn and look toward the center of the glade and see your fellows here. They may not look like they do on Earth; each is a shining being of light who has followed the long path here to learn and celebrate with you. Reach for their hands. Join with them. Dance the sacred dance and sing the sacred song. Raise your voices in magical power.*" (Pause. It sometimes helps to begin an Om-type chant at this juncture. Allow the music to naturally crest and fall.)

"*Now you are ready to go back. Bid your companions farewell and wish them well on their journey. Each of you turns away from the center of the circle and walks back in the direction from which you came.*" (Reverse the journey inward at this point; don't leave out any details.) "*When you reach the temple door, you turn and survey the garden one more time. You understand that this place is yours to come to at will alone or with the group. It will always be here; it will always be open as long as you hold your talisman.*

Step through the doorway and turn to see the door close behind. Notice that the door now has many more talismans than just yours—those of each person who came here. Remove only your own talisman from the door and walk down the avenue toward the stairs. When you arrive at the staircase, you realize that you are sensing the stairs while not actually seeing them. Calmly place your foot on the first stair. Begin the ascent down." (The rest is all repetition, in reverse with a group discussion following.)

VISION QUESTS

Of all the different types of trance and pathwork, a vision quest is perhaps the most serious and taxing. Here, you give yourself over to the Ancestors, spirit guides, or the Divine, seeking insight. Exactly what type of insight depends largely on your quest. Among some Native American cultures' traditions, for example, one vision quest focuses on finding a power animal. Once found, this spiritual creature walks with you as a teacher, protector, and guide. In other shamanic belief systems, people undergo vision quests when they become adults to find a new name suited to their adult role in the community.

Typically, when you undergo a vision quest, you begin by making offerings, saying prayers that indicate intention, taking a ritual bath, and abstaining from foods, sleep, or sexual activity for a pre-specified amount of time (often three days). Once purified in body, mind, and spirit, you may seek the services of a guide or mentor. In many traditions, however, this guide and mentor is chosen by the community or by your family.

Depending on the reason for the vision quest, the guide has several roles to fulfill. It is their job to be sure you have properly prepared yourself. In some cases, the guide does this by actually bathing you, sitting in a sweat lodge and telling traditional stories, or offering sound advice before the ritual begins.

At the outset of the vision quest, the guide or mentor helps set the stage by accompanying you to a prespecified location (often in nature, away from worldly things) and guiding you through a visualization similar to those in pathworking exercises. At some time during the visualization, you're likely to be asked if you still wish to proceed. A vision quest cannot be forced; it must be desired and accepted.

The similarity to pathworking ends, however, once you are past this point and have taken up an abode inside this natural, astral womb. Now you are left alone for a set number of hours or days to find your own way to understanding and to power. If the seeker is a young child, the guardian might opt to stay secretively nearby to watch protectively, but at no point may they interfere with the vision quest's natural progression.

At the end of a vision quest, you may choose to discuss things with an elder, but for the most part, this is a private affair between you and Spirit. It is a vision that will guide and motivate, revealing harsh truths and beautiful wonders. Returning from a vision quest is like being reborn with a refreshed awareness of self, others, Earth, and the universe.

In walking the Adept's Path, you will discover that an understanding of trances, pathworking, and vision quests will help in many ways. These moments between the worlds shed more light on our waking reality so that we can walk the Path of Beauty confidently.

CHAPTER SEVEN
WORKING WITH NATURAL AND ELEMENTAL SPIRITS

"It sounds like stories from the land of spirits."
—Samuel T. Coleridge

In reading old books of magic like the *Key of Solomon*, it is impossible to overlook the number of spells, incantations, rituals, protective measures, and other procedures aimed at calling upon and controlling various types of spirits. Be it a ghost, deva, or the ancient spectral dragon of Arthurian legends, spirits seemed to have fascinated early magi and facilitated many of their requests. Yet this service was not without a cost. Some spirits required sacrifice or offerings; others revolted against the masters who summoned them with dire consequences. With this in mind, I ask that you approach this chapter with all due caution, consideration, and appropriate magical safeguards for everything you undertake.

SPIRITUAL SAFETY

I highly recommend creating a formal sacred space anytime you're planning to work with spirits, even on a cursory level. This invokes the protection of the elemental guardians and your personal god or goddess. It also creates a sphere of energy that contains and helps control the entity until your work is completed.

Begin by calling the Watchtowers in any manner suited to your tradition. Consider bringing a lit white candle into the sacred space to represent the watchful care of your guardian spirits or deities. Also bring a container filled with a mixture of some dried broom flowers or cuttings from your household broom (to sweep away negativity), salt (for cleansing), iron filings (to avert mischievous intentions), rowan (for psychism), garlic (for banishing and protection), rosemary (for purification and safety), and fennel (to keep evil at bay). If you make enough of this and don't mind vacuuming later, you can also sprinkle it around the perimeter of the working area to mark the magic circle. This creates a potent barrier against negative thought forms, or spirits that might have a personal agenda.

Within the boundaries of this sacred space, you have the complete right and wherewithal to tell ill-motivated or uninvited spirits to leave. Don't hesitate to do so. I don't mention this to frighten anyone, but every time you open an astral door, it's highly likely that spirits other than the one you seek will be nearby. If at any time you sense an unwelcome spirit hovering or breaching your wards, toss a pinch of the herb mixture in the direction of this energy and command it to depart. Stay firm in your resolve, focus on the light of the sacred candle and the divine light in your heart, and the spirit will leave you.

Do not, under any circumstances, dismiss the sacred space until you've commanded the invoked spirit back to its point of origin. If you skimp on this step, you're likely to end up with a haunting, poltergeist activity, or mischievous fairies in the working region until you send the spirit back. Consider this spiritual hygiene. Always clean up your magical work!

A GHOST OF A CHANCE

In my tradition of Witchcraft, we believe that all manner of spirits exists in the astral landscape. Among the myriads of residents, we find the souls of deceased people who hover between lives, angels and guides, and elevated souls who choose not to reunite with the Divine in order to help struggling humans along their paths. All of these beings can be contacted through advanced methods. But why call on a ghost or spirit at all?

From a historical standpoint, ancient magi sought out the aid of spirits for three basic reasons. These three goals reflect a strong conviction among our progenitors that the spirit and temporal worlds are closely connected, and that one can affect the other. The first reason was to gain insight into pressing community problems like the spiritual cause of famine or drought and what offerings should be made to reverse the trend. The second was to obtain cures for illnesses believed to have been caused by malevolent spirits.

Finally, our forebears called on spirits to gather information for telling the future. For whatever reason, early people believed that those existing outside the physical realm have a better grasp on what occurred in the past and what's going on in the present, and (by extension) looking into the future in this manner seemed especially common among kings, overlords, and military leaders hoping to wage successful campaigns.

NECROMANCY

By definition, *necromancy* is divination that's accomplished by contacting the spirits of the dead. But it's also often considered any type of magic performed with the aid of a spirit. The original Latin word was *nigromancy,* which implied a dark art, but necromantic procedures are not limited to the left-hand path. For example, Saul (a righteous man) conversed with spirits through the Witch of Endor in First Samuel. Be that as it may, necromancy is a dangerous art, and one that I do not really recommend even to adepts.

Consider that most spirits in the nether realms have to reincarnate meaning they still have flaws and are prone to personal opinions and agendas much as they were in mortal life. Some spirits don't take kindly to being forced to bend to a magus's will. And there's always the possibility of figuratively dialing the wrong astral number. You could end up getting completely incorrect information, half-truths, the wrong ghost, or an angry spirit that will want to vent its ire in your direction!

If you feel it necessary to call upon a spirit, please take the proper precautions and remember:

- Know the spirit upon which you're calling, especially its true name. By using this name, you can banish the spirit should it prove ill-mannered.
- Don't use just any procedure you find in an old book for calling up spirits. Some of the medieval grimoires, for example, were written by those who sought to undermine magical traditions and contain completely false presentations. Instead, I suggest asking advice from someone who has practiced High Magic for some years. You can certainly create your own calling ritual but do so *after* you've gained

as much knowledge as possible into traditional necromantic procedures.
- Keep the purpose of the summoning in mind all the while you work.
- Pose your question or behest quickly. Don't make the spirit tarry any longer than necessary.
- If the spirit cooperates, thank it kindly just as you would anyone that helped you. Courtesy is appreciated by spirits, too.

As soon as the spirit has performed the task for which you called it, say goodbye and let it (or command it to) return from whence it came. Wait until the energy of that spirit is completely gone, then close the circle.

As always, make notes of your experiences. If for any reason you sense that a spirit has lingered after a ritual, use cleansing and purifying rites from your personal tradition to send it back. About the only time these methods don't work is when you've contacted a ghost (an Earth-bound spirit) that has been in that region for some time. Such a ghost may be fettered to the location or be working out some uncompleted task from life. Unless this ghost is causing trouble, it might be better (and more interesting) to leave it alone.

MEDIUMSHIP

Mediumship has some potential drawbacks—namely the temporary relinquishing of the body so spirits can speak through it—but it is generally considered to be safer than necromancy. By definition, a *medium* is someone who acts as an intermediary between this world and the next by transmitting various communications. Mediums accomplish this by adjusting every cell of their bodies temporarily to accept the frequency of a specific spirit or thought form from the astral. They then transmit this frequency somewhat like a radio.

Most people who become mediums already have a sensitivity to spirits. This particular gift makes it much easier to find, contact, and then speak to a ghost or spirit. If deemed necessary, mediums can then choose to let the spirit speak through them. Additionally, effective mediums have strong wills and the ability to control their astral selves. This allows them to stand at the ready to take over the situation if a spirit begins giving erroneous or negative messages. If you do not already possess these two abilities, I strongly suggest developing them more fully before attempting mediumship.

The exact procedure for mediumship often varies by the individual practitioner. You may have to try several different methods to hit on what's right for you. This makes sense considering the personal nature of most magical traditions and the fact that it's your body being given over.

The good news is that at least one similarity exists in almost all contacts with the spirit world. Specifically, most mediums have a ritual of sorts that they perform before an attempt to contact a spirit. They may pray, wash their hands, fast, meditate, light candles, pull out certain tools (like a crystal ball), and the like. Whatever the tool or procedure you decide upon, this time is very important; it creates the mindset, trance state, and environment necessary for communion with spirits.

From this point forward, only you can really express how you find and communicate with a specific entity. The way our minds interpret a spiritual presence and then interact with that presence is unique to each individual. One medium might notice an aroma in the air that signals a ghostly presence and then follow their nose (somewhat literally) to the source. Another medium might actually see a vision of a person in their mind's eye and talk to that image directly.

No matter the spiritual and sensual cues you discover signaling contact, once a spirit comes, you must then decide whether or not to allow the entity to speak through you. Don't rush this decision. Do whatever you can to ensure that the spirit either is the one you wished to contact or is a good-intentioned entity before you jump into rapport.

If you move forward, how the merger of human and spirit occurs is, again, very personal. The medium who followed the aroma might feel that scent becoming part of them, mingling with personal perfumes or colognes. The medium who saw the image might envision the spirit's portrait blending with their own. Whatever the approach, this blended merger remains in place until the spirit is done communicating or until you break contact.

At this juncture, slowly return your breathing to its normal pace and reestablish conscious awareness. Seriously consider having a discussion afterward about the information received. Some people, once in the trance state, are not able to hear or integrate the spirit's message. This discussion will allow both you and the participants to benefit more fully from the experience.

Come the end of this discussion period (or during it), remind those gathered that information from spirits is fallible, except in the rare instances when you contact a master teacher. Consequently, all the participants (including the medium) should balance the experience against what their inner voice says, keeping what seems viable and leaving the rest by the wayside. Truth, if it is indeed truth, will always come back through unrelated sources later.

OF NATURE, MYTH, AND MAGIC

In some magical traditions, the power of mythical or spirit creatures is called upon to guard the sacred space, assist with spells, energize and guide rituals, or offer insights. At first, we may find this idea odd or implausible—that is, until we remind ourselves that within the sacred circle there is no time, no dimension, no reality that is outside our reach.

Consider how long creatures like the dragon and unicorn have existed in humankind's communal thoughts. Even if these beasts never existed, the length of time people have been writing, talking, and musing about them creates a thought form that we can call upon in a magical setting. Consider, too, how long folks practicing shamanic rites have been seeking out animal spirits as teachers, guides, and protectors. The sheer "ancientness" of these types of practices gives them an incredible amount of potential for advanced studies.

LEGENDARY ENERGY

Throughout the world, we find accounts of fantastic animals whose magical powers were as great as their stories. In the astral landscape such creatures may run freely, and if we treat these powers with respect, they can help us in our magic. For example, rather than calling the usual elemental powers to guard the sacred circle, conjure the spirit of a red dragon in the South for protection. The Northern quarter might be guarded by a satyr spirit, the Western regions by a sea serpent, and the Eastern portion by a roc.

Alternatively, consider calling on such spirits when you need understanding and awareness in specific areas of your life. For example, when you can see no way to recoup a loss, call on the phoenix to show you how to rise above circumstances. To rid yourself of an overwhelming burden from the past, call on the albatross.

Finally, you may politely invoke these powers for specific tasks similarly to any other spirit but make sure the task assigned makes sense considering the creature. Pegasus or a griffon, for example, would make a speedy messenger. The latter delivers harsher missives, however, due to its nature. A sphinx is suited to watching over and protecting anything you cherish for a specific period of time. A gnome can help you improve your finances by finding the proverbial treasures that surround you every day, and a fairy might be asked to teach someone how to reconnect with the playful portion of self instead of being so serious all the time.

As a side note, when creatures like this begin showing up in your dreams, in advertisements that you see often, on logos, or the like, this may be an omen or message from the beast to you, to a community, or to Earth. For example, for a while unicorns were very popular. This creature came to us representing the need to reclaim some of humankind's lost innocence—the ability to believe like children in wonders and love again. Similarly, the recent emergence of angels symbolizes our need to reconnect with the Sacred.

So, should you notice a sudden glut of mythical beasts appearing in your life or society, look over the following list of commonly mentioned legendary animals and see what the creature is saying. You can also use this list to help you choose what type of mythical spirit is best to help you with the magic at hand:

- *Albatross (a bird that is sacred to seafarers):* The albatross represents a wrong that needs to be rectified so that you—or society—can move forward liberated from the weight of the past. It also gently

reminds us that some memories are meant to be cherished and learned from, while others should be left behind.
- *Brownie (a shaggy fairy that adopts a home, protects it, and often helps with little tasks like brewing):* These industrious creatures symbolize the value of and rewards from doing a job well and being considerate of others. In stories, they always help humans with kindly natures who treat them respectfully and are forever attending to various tasks that would otherwise remain incomplete.
- *Centaur (man-horse):* In Greek mythology, some centaurs accompany heroes, while others are wild and lawless. Here we see the duality that everyone faces between light and dark, courage and fear, society and the wild person within. Additionally, due to the centaur's association with the constellation Sagittarius (the archer), it may symbolize the need to figuratively hit a mark or pursue a goal.
- *Chimera (lion's head, goat's body):* The world of imagination, creativity, illusion and wonder. A chimera's appearance can signal the beginning of an inventive spurt. Alternatively, it can act as a warning that something is hidden from you right now, so look more closely.
- *Dragon:* Dragons represent power for boon or bane. Some people abuse power and overcome others with their strength, while other folks use it to help. So, what's your dragon doing? Dragons often bear messages about magical studies, the way we communicate (note the fire-breathing dragons), and matters requiring wisdom. They often choose to act as protectors of bards and others who guard and remember our sacred stories.

- *Earth tortoise or whale:* In several different traditions, Earth rests on the back of a great creature that guides it safely on its course through the sky. This beast represents our need to reconnect with nature and its cycles more intimately. It may also symbolize universal brother- and sisterhood, and the wonders of the stars that still await us.
- *Elf:* Also known as *shining beings,* the elves bear a strong association with our dreamtime and messages that come while we sleep.
- *Gnome (small earth-dwelling fairies often believed to be the guards of buried treasure):* The word *gnome* comes in part from a Greek root word meaning "knowledge." In essence, these beings often appear to spur conscious learning and reasoning. Being Earth dwellers, the gnomes also presage financial improvements, often those that result from steadfast efforts.
- *Griffon (eagle's head on a lion's body):* Dante portrays these beasts as drawing a triumphant chariot which gives them the symbolism of success and victory. In legend, griffons often guard treasures, so they may signal a personal or global discovery of great import.
- *Hydra:* A horrid beast with eight or nine heads, the hydra speaks to us of scattering our attention in too many directions or proverbially having "too many cooks" on a project. Additionally, hydras were said to have the power of regeneration. If you feel nearly defeated, then this being offers the hope of recuperation.
- *Merpeople:* Beings of enchantment and emotion, they often symbolize matters of intuition or the heart. Since merpeople are closely attuned with

the Water element, they can also teach us how to swim in difficult waters or to flow peacefully through life's course.
- *Naga (half-human and half-serpent being):* Powerful tricksters, nagas offer strength to those they favor but also remind us that not all things are what they seem.
- *Pegasus (winged horse):* Strength, courage, and devotion to a cause are all characteristic of this beast, which was sacred to the Greek goddess Athena.
- *Phoenix (the bird that nests in a roaring fire and is reborn by it):* The ancient alchemical symbol of immortality and transmutation. You are about to find a way to make something good out of a seemingly bad situation and come out far better in the process.
- *Satyr:* A playful, sometimes mischievous earth spirit, the satyr attempts to waken the child within who loves to dance among trees, jump in mud puddles, and generally revel in simple pleasures. In some cases, the appearance of a satyr may signal prophetic abilities beginning to evidence themselves, such as having a dream that comes true or a flash of insight that a friend needs your help when you know nothing of the situation in advance.
- *Siren:* A warning that the tempting situation before you (especially a relationship) may not be in your best interest. Get some emotional distance before making any quick decisions.
- *Sphinx (woman's head, lion's body, tail of a serpent, wings of an eagle):* Finding the answer to a plaguing enigma or riddle. Also, the union of mind and body to comprehend and use the powers given us by nature.

- *Sylph:* Sylphs are masters of magic and often appear to give humans a healthy nudge in discovering the magical self. Additionally, sylphs have a powerful affinity with nature and Air elements and therefore are good helpmates in Air magic.
- *Thunderbird:* An omen of forthcoming war or blessings.

TOTEMS AND GUIDES

Spirit animals appear frequently in shamanic and indigenous cultures and have been adopted by many non-indigenous people who see spirit animals as the perfect vehicle for living a more Earth-aware life. When we talk about spirit animals in all forms, be mindful of closed practices, respectful of the relationship's serious nature, and share in these creatures' wisdom; don't take what isn't yours.

A totem is a spirit animal with which one develops a special rapport analogous to having a family member in the astral landscape. Stressing this deep connection, the term *totem* comes from the Ojibwa word *ototeman*, the Algonquian *nto'te-m*, or the Cree *ototema*, all of which mean "kin." It is not something you simply identify yourself with on a surface level. The methods of discovering your totem vary from tradition to tradition, but the overall approach seems to be analogous to a vision quest. Generally, you prepare yourself physically and spiritually through bathing, fasting, and prayer. You then go to a natural setting, leave out a small token gift suitable to the creature with which you're communing (if known), induce a trance state, and wait to see what visions (if any) develop.

Any ensuing vision reveals the animal guide, its powers, and its reasons for being present at this time through the way the animal behaves or through telepathic or empathic communication. For example, a person who has suffered lifelong fearfulness might discover a lion totem that comes specifically to protect and teach courage. A person who's overly stoic may discover a playful otter standing by, encouraging a more frolicsome attitude, and one who has trouble with honest communications could discover a spirit owl that flies with the potent wings of truthfulness.

If you decide to undergo a quest like this, please release yourself from any preconceived notions about what your personal totem may be. There are no limits to what type of spirit animal could appear, and many shamanic traditions hold that each person has several of these powerful beings to aid in various facets of life. Also, some people believe that plants, stones, and even mythic creatures can fulfill this role. I happen to agree, but this is not a conventional view.

Once a totemic relationship develops, the spirit animal goes with you everywhere as a guardian, teacher, and a stern censor when you stray. Some people develop an empathic rapport with their spirit animals' Earth-bound representatives. For example, those with raven totems may find they begin understanding bird whistles on a deeply intuitive level. Because of such gifts from the spirit totem, it is appropriate to have an artistic rendering of it nearby to honor its influence in your life.

No matter what type of totem you discover, it is considered abhorrent to kill or harm any natural manifestation of it. This is analogous to harming a trusting, helpful sibling. Such a thoughtless deed ruins your relationship with this power until the damage is somehow rectified, or the spirit somehow appeased through offerings, prayers, or a personal quest of atonement.

It should also be noted that the rapport and relationship between you and any spirit animal can change dramatically over time. This transformation reflects the changes experienced in your life and spiritual path. Indeed, during times of drastic change, you may discover one spirit animal leaving and another taking its place. When this occurs (and I can almost guarantee it will), bid your old friend farewell and thank it for its help. Welcome the new spirit totem and guide and get to know it just as intimately as the previous presence.

In working with a totem, remember that, somewhat like familiars, totems can become effective spiritual partners in all you do if you let them. They will not overstep the boundaries of free will; you have to open an astral doorway anytime you wish for the creature's aid, advice, or energy to achieve certain goals. Return the spirit totem's respectful demeanor by never treating it like a servant or a child and never taking it for granted. Such actions can cause serious difficulties between you and your totem.

As long as you honor your totem and appreciate its efforts on your behalf (including the harsh lessons it may bring), you'll find this relationship extremely gratifying. Since the totem lives in the astral, it can help you traverse this realm with greater efficacy and sometimes act as an intermediary between you and other indwelling spirits. It can also provide you with insights and perspectives that daily corporeal living doesn't afford, similar to the elementals in the section that follows. You should not try to anticipate what type of animal guide might come to you. What appears will be what you most need in your life. If you don't like the creature, it may reflect deep-seated fears or self-doubts that desperately need your attention and rectification. Of course, you could just ignore the totem, but this would be a terrible insult to the spirit, which would never come to you again.

ELEMENTAL SPIRITS

"One gift the fairies gave me (three they commonly bestowed of yore) the love of books, the golden key that opens the enchanted door."
— Andrew Lang

When you begin practicing magic, one of the first things you learn is that everything on the planet has a specific elemental correspondence—all things are aligned with Earth, Air, Fire, Water, or Spirit (ether). These associations create the foundations for the way plants, stones, and the like are used in many spells, charms, and rituals. This is a very good foundation for elemental magic.

As adepts will tell you, however, a true mastery of the elements goes far beyond knowing these associations. It comes from an awareness of the beings that reside in each element and knowing how to work with these powers harmoniously for specific goals. This is not a simple task, nor one that is wholly safe.

Elementals are beings of raw drive—beings who are so strongly connected to nature or one specific element that comprehending their motives and ways is very difficult for even the most advanced magical students. While an adept might know how to summon an elemental for a task, knowing whether it will accept the task (and if so, *why*) is another matter altogether. And it's generally considered very poor form to command or willfully coerce an elemental. Even if such brazenness works, the person so doing may cause the elemental to become a potent adversary that is likely to retaliate when given an opportunity.

So, in reading the section that follows and in all your elemental work, bear in mind the following:

- It is best to try calling and working with elemental powers within the confines of a sacred circle. This way, if something goes awry, you don't end up having an elemental on the loose in your house, which causes no end of difficulty. People with errant water elementals, for example, might discover ongoing problems with dripping faucets and leaky pipes.
- Elementals are powerful energy sources deserving of respect. They are also among your best helpmates for learning how to control an element and use it effectively for magic. So, treat them as you would any valued teacher and ally.
- If you're concerned about or don't feel ready for working with elementals, try making an elementary instead (see below). This energy source is designed for one purpose and doesn't have the willful nature of an elemental.

Working with Elementals

Just like people, elementals have characteristics, habits, likes, and dislikes. The type of task you give an elemental needs to be suited to its specific qualities. So, before calling on an elemental, it's good to know the kind of personality you're dealing with.

Air elementals are capricious, meaning that they can get sidetracked easily or potentially weave a little humor into a given task. Even so, Air elementals can traverse great distances quickly, making them effective messengers. Air is also a good, gentle motivator for fortune (think of the "wind at your back") and puts luck into motion.

Earth elementals tend to be very set in their ways. They can't travel far without losing potency. But when it comes to building strong foundations, putting down roots, and security, an Earth elemental can't be beat.

Fire elementals experience bursts of energy (both good and bad) and may burn themselves out before a task is completed if you don't build and tend the birthing fires carefully. These elementals need guarded control so they don't accidentally set the world on fire (literally). On the other hand, Fire elementals energize, impassion, warm, and generally stimulate change where stagnation dwells.

Finally, Water elementals splash full of emotion, which can lead them more strongly than your request. The fluid nature of Water elementals allows them to get into areas that an Earth elemental couldn't, but they also have no real backbone. Water's power is in its ability to wear away at walls, release pent-up feelings, awaken the spiritual nature, and overcome creative blockage.

In your work with elementals, knowing this basic information from the get-go helps you work more effectively. Now you understand the elementals' quirks and can appeal to their natural characteristics when asking for help. This also ensures that you choose the right elemental for the task at hand.

For example, Fire is fine for nurturing passion but not the best choice for long-term relationships because it burns out. Earth, on the other hand, is good for relationships; it creates a rich foundation. Someone afraid of commitment, however, will be frightened off by Earth elemental energy. Water frees up emotional blockage but can sometimes be overwhelming. Air is the proverbial free spirit that never wants to be tied down. Think carefully about what elemental energy is best for your magical goal before proceeding to call one into the circle.

Calling an Elemental

Unlike spirits or ghosts, you do not command an elemental—you invite it. Begin by setting up your sacred space so that everything therein somehow honors and welcomes the desired elemental. Here's a brief list of objects, herbs, and stones that might be used in summoning each elemental type:

- *Earth:* Plain stones, rich soil, seeds, green and brown items, grains, cotton, patchouli incense, potted flowers, root crops (carrots, potatoes, radishes), green agate, green tourmaline, turquoise, jet.
- *Air:* A handheld or electric fan, an open window, pastel-colored items, dandelions, maple leaves, bells and wind chimes, pine or sage incense, rice, mica, pumice, aventurine.
- *Fire:* A candle, pilot light, or fireplace, red and orange items, hot foods (peppers and the like), mint incense, oak leaves, juniper, cedar, amber, red agate, lava stone, bloodstone.
- *Water:* A bowl or glass of water, seashells, sand, blue or blue-green items, cool foods (cucumber, grapes, and so on), daisy, heather, myrrh, willow, blue lace agate, aquamarine, coral, jade, lapis.

Next, call the quarters, making a special invocation to the directional power in which the desired elemental resides. Sit in the center of the circle in direct contact with one or more of the symbolic tokens you chose to honor the elemental. In your mind, extend a greeting and welcome, stating your purpose (like learning how to use a particular elemental energy more effectively in magic), then wait. If an elemental chooses to respond, it will signal its presence somehow. Water elemental may bring a slight damp feeling to the air or signal you by making waves in the container of water. Earth elementals feel heavy as if gravity is stronger and you're very connected to the Mother. Fire elementals are warm and may bring air static with them. Air elementals come on a wind or in your body's breath.

Once the elemental arrives, give it your request with all due expediency. It will either accept the task or say no. Whatever the elemental's choice, thank it courteously for coming and let it return to its natural environment as soon as possible. The elemental needs to return to the astral landscape to accomplish what you've asked; it can't do so from the temporal. While an elemental's presence can be felt on the earthly plane and it affects this reality, the real power of this being is etheric.

After the elemental leaves, take time to write in your magical journal about the experience. Pay particular attention to the cues the elemental used to signal its presence and how it communicated to you (often via empathy or telepathy). Also note whether or not you feel it accepted the task, and what if any results came from the effort. This last point will help you better gauge what jobs elementals will, and will not, accept in planning future attempts.

Making and Controlling Elementaries

An *elementary* is a personally devised miniature elemental that has deep, penetrating energy. Elementaries are designed for accomplishing specific tasks; each must be given a name to complete its task, and the elements used in creating it must be suited to this task. Since you are the sole creator of the elementary and give it life, it will be much easier to control and guide than pure elementals. In this manner, your will blends with element and energy to create a driven magical force that mirrors your desire.

Simple elementaries are created by projecting one (or several) elements from the earth into a ready-made shape (a body of sorts), like a bowl. If the elementary is for personal use only, you can project the energy from yourself into the shape for greater empathy. Try to choose a shape that symbolically represents the elements being used since this object will become the interim housing for your elementary when it returns from a task. For example, bowls and glasses are suited to Water elementaries, while a plant pot might be better for an Earth elementary. Also choose permanent housing for the elementary (like a clock, a bracelet, or something else that other people don't handle) so it has a house in which to rest after it comes back.

Place a pinch of the base element(s), such as soil or a seed for Earth, a drop for Water, a feather for Air, and ashes or a match for Fire, into this shape. Again, make sure the elements you use are suited to the task. Air elementaries, for example, make excellent message bearers and motivators, while Fire elementaries literally put a fire under stagnating projects.

Focus your attention and will on the task (like seeking a lost item or helping to locate new magickal friends) and the elementary you're creating. Willfully fill the form with energy. Keep your spiritual eyes and ears open so you can "see" the elementary forming. Continue projecting energy and desire into the shape until you sense a kind of personality with you in the room. At this point, the elementary must be given a name or it will die. The elementary also can be given a specific life span, one reasonable considering the tasks you want this creature to accomplish. Some elementaries can last a lifetime, while others need only live for a few hours.

Reach into the shape and take the elementary in hand. Whisper your task once more to the creature (keeping this uncomplicated), order its return to home upon completion, then send it on its way. At this point, return to your normal everyday tasks. Don't focus on the elementary because the empathy between you and it may interfere with the given task. Also, leave the elementary's shape open and untouched while it's away. This is the housing to which the creature returns when the task is done.

One way to know if your elementary has returned, if you're not psychically or intuitively aware of it, is by pendulum divination, dowsing, or another binary divination system. When any of these methods tells you the creature is home, send the elementary to its chosen permanent house and wrap the object used to create its body (the shape) with black silk to protect that energy. Only unwrap the shape when you wish to recharge the elementary or when you wish to send it out again. Note, however, that if you've given the elementary a life span, the energy in the shape dissipates at the end of that span, too.

To make an elementary that's suited to more difficult tasks, begin with a beeswax and aloe doll four or more inches tall. Make an opening in the top of the doll using a pencil or screwdriver and fill this opening with liquid (wine is a good choice). To personalize this elementary, add a bit of your saliva, sweat, or tears to the wine. Seal the opening with more beeswax.

Hold the figurine in your non-dominant hand, rub it with your dominant hand, breathe into it with the winds of life, and give it a name. Empower the elementary by filling its loins with Earth energy, its abdomen with Water energy, its cheek with Air energy, and its Head with fire energy. Once you're done, concentrate all your will toward the elementary's head and focus on the attributes you want the creature to have.

Envision the being as filled with universal light. Let this pour down and saturate the wax and wine until it's overflowing. As this is being accomplished, also fix the date of the elementary's death in your mind so that a life span is established.

Breathe into the wax once more, saying, *"live."* Wrap the doll in black silk until you need to call upon the elementary to fulfill a task. While it's wrapped—and, in fact, at all other times—no one but you should handle the doll. When you remove it for an errand, dress it in colors or clothing suited to the task, then charge the elementary with its job through ritual, will, and visualization. Leave the black cloth off the doll until the elementary returns, then wrap it again, storing it safely and securely.

Take care to store the figurine in a cool area. If the wax begins to melt or is damaged in any way, it can kill the elementary or warp the energy you've placed therein. Should this happen, it's best to unmake the elementary (reversing the process) and destroy the doll so that your magic doesn't go awry.

A third method of creating elementaries comes from Tibet. Before beginning you will need to decide the gender, name, life span, and a binding spot (a doll or object) for the elementary. Also determine where it will be stored upon completion. This should be a spot known only to you; no one else should handle the finished housing.

Next, take a large piece of paper and draw a circle on it. Inside the circle, inscribe two interlocking squares so they form an eight-pointed star. This represents the balance of all four elements in all their positive and negative aspects. Draw an emblem that represents the elementary you're about to create (different traditions have different representations for the elements—choose one that has personal meaning for you) at the center point of the octagram. Then, on a small, round piece of metal, like a coin or slug (half an inch in diameter), engrave the same series of symbols using any sharp implement. This metal goes at the core of the large diagram and becomes a temporary housing for the elementary during its creation.

Give the elementary a name and call to it. Inhale the element(s) that will abide in and energize the elementary, then direct this power into the center point of your diagrams. Similarly, direct your will and desires into this point to animate the elementary. Continue the flow of elemental power and direct your will until you feel nearly exhausted.

Now send the elementary to its storage place, binding the piece of metal to that shape or object. Fold the large paper and wrap this in black silk. Use the large paper anytime you want to recharge the elementary. Detach and hold the small metal talisman in your hand each time you give the elementary an order. You may even want to keep the metal with you until the elementary completes the task. This maintains your empathic connection.

At the end of an elementary's life, its paper and metal should not be reused for making new elementaries (think of this as akin to wearing clothes from a corpse). Ritually destroy or bury these items so that the elementary has an honorable "grave." This also neatly cleans up any residual psychic energy that the paper and metal may bear, even without the elementary's presence.

Because we are mortal beings who live within time, there are certainly circumstances under which working with spirits can prove very helpful and insightful. Nonetheless, it is not something to try haphazardly, just for fun, without training, or without adequate protection. In our pursuit of adepthood we need to wisely use the resources we have but not abuse them or treat them lightly. The lessons learned this way, and the resulting insights—both become valuable companions in serving our communities, as seen in the next chapter.

CHAPTER EIGHT
SERVING THE COMMUNITY

"Love and compassion are necessities, not luxuries. Without them humanity cannot survive."

—The Dalai Lama

While it might be tempting for adepts to live a hermetic lifestyle, few of us can (or do) exist in a vacuum. We all have communities that we belong to: family, friends, work, a town or city, any magical groups with which we interact, and the community of Earth. Each of these neighborhoods is affected by the magic we create. As adepts or elders, we remain culpable for the results that come from these metaphysical efforts, and we are also entrusted with new tasks: teaching, healing, counseling, monitoring, and generally working magic for our communities.

Service is a means of giving back something. Since Witches don't exactly tithe, community service effectively shows thankful appreciation to the Divine and the universe for our blessings. It is also an effective approach for externally portraying Witchcraft in a positive, proactive manner. This chapter, therefore, examines some of the ways in which you can begin serving your communities as you grow along your path toward mastery.

Teaching

In days of old, a young person would go to a master and ask to become an apprentice. This kind of teaching program—where individuals gently guide and instruct other individuals—still exists in the magical community, but it is not without questions and conundrums. For example, how do you know for certain whom you should or should not teach? How many students do you accept at a time? What should you do when someone you're interviewing displays improper motivation?

As a writer, I receive numerous requests to teach, so I know how hard it is to say no. But neither you nor I can teach everyone who asks. First and foremost, the people you accept as students need to have a similar view of magic and the universe for the student-teacher relationship to work effectively. Besides this, students should also display:

- A sense of spiritual independence. In other words, they will listen to your advice and ponder it seriously but not look to you as an infallible guru.
- A sense of respect balanced with empathy toward the teacher. Vital to a healthy student-teacher relationship is the understanding that both individuals are fallible humans who have real needs and real shortcomings. This means neither party will take advantage of the other purposefully and neither will feel deceived when inevitable failures or problems come.

- An honest desire to learn, including healthy curiosity, sensible caution, attentiveness, and a willingness to give up some free time for the Craft. Give prospective students a few projects with specific instructions and deadlines and see how they do with them.
- A good balance between spiritual vision and mundane reality. If a student's family, for example, has a pressing need, do they call and ask for an extension on an assignment? If so, this is a good sign. On the other hand, watch out for repeat excuse makers.
- An understanding that they, not you, are the master of personal fate, and that magic is a helpmate, not a crutch for personal development.
- A proper motivation and attitude for learning magical arts. Watch for significant warning signs in prospective students' personality like vanity, power tripping, insecurity, immaturity, apathy, gossip mongering, pessimism, and intolerance. If prospective students brag about whom they know in the magical community, for example, it's definitely a bad sign. Conversely, sometimes taking students like this under your wing provides an opportunity for them to transform their negative thought patterns and behaviors that they may not have had previously.
- An understanding from the get-go that this relationship may or may not be long lasting. Some student-teacher bonds last forever, but at some point, the student should also "grow up" and become a teacher. In other cases, students must be released (or even cut off) so they can grow to personal fullness.
- An awareness that they (the students) also have valuable insights to share in the process of learning.

> Sometimes a fresh outlook is just the right medicine to cure a case of magical stagnation. No question, except the one that remains unasked, is "dumb." No concept is silly except that which remains unexplored.

Once you've decided to accept a student, then the process of education begins. The first thing I tell students is not to believe a word I say. This surprises them but gives me the chance to discuss individuals' roles in their own magical education. We cannot carve other people's paths out for them. A teacher's role is that of a guide, not an overlord.

Despite this example, there's no exact "right" way to embark on the student-teacher path. The correct genesis depends a lot on your students' level of knowledge, skill, and learning pace, as well as your teaching methods. Take each step slowly until you get a good feel for each of these facets in the relationship. Don't push for too much too soon, especially on the level of trust, or some really unpleasant situations may result.

Additionally, it's important to remember that you are fundamentally responsible for each of your students' magic for as long as they study with you. When one of them messes up, your job becomes one of damage control and stern admonishment. If you're uncomfortable with either role, don't teach. Find another way to serve your communities.

Public Education

The New Age movement has done much to further the Craft and give it some mainstream support. Even so, undoing two thousand years of misinformation isn't easy. There are many people around the world who do not understand the Craft or what really constitutes a magical lifestyle. Part of this confusion is generated by the visionary, personalized aspect of the Craft, and the rest comes from misrepresentation in the media, churches, and from zealous individuals within our community who have good intentions but little wisdom.

So, public education is very important. It is long past time to undo the heinous representations of Witchcraft and show our true colors. This doesn't mean throwing stones back in the direction from which they came, which often happens as a knee-jerk reaction. Instead, it means communicating about and living our magic without apology.

Yes, there are times when discretion is necessary, but we are hopefully working toward a time when it won't be. So many religions in the world openly express their beliefs in symbolic clothing or jewelry, actions, holiday observances, and the like. Wear a pentagram or say "Gods bless" to someone and see what happens! Similarly, about the only time Witches get interviewed is on Halloween. These are the kinds of stereotypes that the leaders in our community have a chance to dispel, but it's going to take time and effort.

If you're comfortable with talking to people, one way you can approach this is to get together with representatives of the media in your area. Offer to help with occult-related stories so that at the least, *both* sides of the issue get exposure. Send information to local influencers and major community members. And when inaccurate representations of the Craft come up, say or do something about it! Being Wiccan or Pagan doesn't mean we can't be resolute about our right to freedom of religion.

Speak the truth, keeping a cool head and maturity as helpful companions. Don't communicate with flowery words or jargon; just talk to people using terms they can readily relate to. Try to be patient in the process.

Becoming more publicly and politically active are two essential factors to the establishment process, as is reeducating people about what it truly means to be a Witch. While we do not feel the need to convert others or wear our faith like a neon sign, the path to improvement begins by opening up our broom closets for close scrutiny and stepping bravely out into society. Of all people suited to this task, elders and adepts offer the greatest amount of wisdom and insight (without the hype). One such group that worked to this end was the former Witches Anti-Defamation League.

So, as you grow, learn, and reach new levels of spiritual maturity, begin sharing your path *with* the people around you. Slowly help them to see how your life is changing for the better. Let your life become an act of worship and a teaching tool so that the words *Witch* and *magic* are no longer something to fear but something of which to be proud.

STUDY GROUPS

Study groups offer a very productive way to share ideas with like-minded people. While most study groups have a designated leader, everyone has an opportunity to participate. From this roundtable-type forum, you can teach what you've learned but also benefit from other people's successful notions and unique insights.

In setting up a study group, several things need to be considered:

- What is the focus of the group? Wicca? Witchcraft? Paganism? General spirituality? Define the goals so that people with similar study aims will be drawn to the group.

- How often will the group meet? These days, it's hard to get people together much more frequently than bimonthly because of work schedules and other commitments.
- When will the group meet? Weekends are easiest, but they're also the time folks want to be with their families. Weeknights eliminate this conflict, but meetings should be set to start early enough that people can be fresh for work (or whatever their schedules look like) the next day.
- Where will the study group meet? I suggest a rotating system so all members get to host the group on a regular basis. This way, no one person is constantly left with the duties of preparation and cleanup.
- What should members bring with them to each meeting? Both pens and paper and smartphones for audio recording and notes are highly recommended, as are some munchies and beverages to share. The foodstuffs decrease the financial burden on the host or hostess and are a good way of honoring the hearth god or goddess in each home you visit.
- What are the general ground rules for the group once the session begins? Nearly every group I've ever participated in had gentle ways of handling nonproductive tangents, urgent needs, disruptions, and so on. Since all these types of situations *will* develop at some point or another, agree ahead of time upon what course of action to take.
- What subject(s) will be covered in each meeting? The topics should be firmed up with all participants before the meeting so people can bring relevant questions and ideas for the discussion.
- Finally, how long will each meeting last? This is important for individuals with babysitters or tight

schedules. I generally suggest two hours, of which thirty minutes is reserved for questions and general fellowship. People who don't have commitments for the following day can always go out for coffee afterward and chat more.

GATHERINGS AND LECTURES

Another great way to share and exchange knowledge with people is by attending gatherings and giving (or listening to) lectures on various topics. Pagan and New Age gatherings host numerous skilled individuals whose knowledge ranges from Buddhist meditation techniques and tantric yoga to the magical language of flowers—and everything in between! Additionally, these gatherings often include several elders and adepts whose life experiences empower, motivate, and inspire those walking the same path.

If you'd like to offer lectures at an event, contact the regional representative noted for the gathering and express your interest. Provide the representative with an overview of the classes you have available, a list of previous experience and qualifications, the names of a few people who could act as references, and what (if any) requirements you have for lecturing. This last point is important. If you need housing, some form of financial compensation, special equipment for the lecture, or anything to support your teaching, all of this can affect the event's budget and planning and should be disclosed beforehand.

The event's representatives use all the information you provide to determine whether or not to include you on the schedule, so present yourself professionally. Once you receive confirmation of your participation, get a list of dates, times, and topics from the coordinators so you can be prepared and prompt for your presentation. In terms of preparation, make an outline of what you want to teach, perhaps photocopy some notes for those who attend, and make sure to pack any items necessary for demonstrations if applicable.

When you write up your outline, bear in mind that you will have individuals with diverse levels of experience gathered into one room for the lecture. Try to find materials that can satisfy nearly any attendee. Also, consider ways to get the attendees talking and participating in the lecture regularly. Humor can be a great ally in teaching and getting people to open up, as can body language. I often sit on the floor when I teach because it's less formal and often dispenses pretense.

Some gathering representatives may ask you to put together customized material to fit a theme. When this occurs, find a subject in your area of expertise that's suitable. Don't try to learn a whole new art just for the event—your lecture would reflect the inexperience. Teach what you *know* and you will rarely fall short of expectations.

Remember that there is no such thing as "Pagan standard time" when you're a speaker. Events have tight schedules that need to be closely adhered to out of consideration for the coordinators, other speakers, and the people who've paid to attend the event. So, other than a five-minute leeway afforded to people who might not be able to find your lecture room, be punctual (even if this is a magical space, wear a watch and use it!).

At the beginning of your lecture, introduce yourself. Tell those assembled a little bit about why you're teaching this subject and what it means to you. Thank them for coming to the conference and make any announcements that the representatives request at this time. This is what I call my time out for public service proclamations, and I've found that it really helps break the ice, especially when you're a little nervous.

Try to leave time at the end of your lecture for questions and socializing. This helps with clarification and integration. Also, some people won't ask questions publicly but will approach you privately afterward with queries. If the room is needed for another speaker, take these people politely outside to another area where you can talk freely. Unless you have to go directly into another lecture or commitment, try to take time for each person so that everyone leaves feeling fulfilled and satisfied.

If, for any reason, you must cancel a scheduled lecture, try to do so as early as possible. Smaller gatherings depend heavily on every speaker and will need lead time to replace you. Larger gatherings aren't so dependent, but they certainly appreciate the courtesy of a phone call or letter explaining the situation. This allows the coordinators to change the programs, advertising, and the like before the event and decrease confusion.

COVENS

Witches traditionally gather in covens: groups that have agreed to assemble for the purpose of working magic together, usually that of a specific tradition. Sounds simple enough, but the recipe for success is anything but simple. Like any group, covens experience interpersonal dynamics and difficulties. Consequently, people thinking about forming a coven need to seriously consider this decision and all the potential problems and responsibilities that go with it.

A *really* good coven leader needs to be magically skilled, organized, somewhat motherly, firm, authoritative, motivational, a good listener, modest, discreet, honorable, sensitive to energy shifts, and very patient. If you find yourself lacking in these kinds of qualities, go ahead and help organize a coven, but don't lead it. Find another person suited to the role.

In a way, organizing an effective coven is like making pastry. Each ingredient (or, in this case, each individual) must be carefully chosen for quality and measured accurately, or else the recipe fails. Too much or too little of specific personality traits can make or break the harmonious flavor and texture of the whole. So, in assembling prospective coven members, think quality and balance, not quantity.

I've seen many groups that play the numbers game for status, wanting to have more members than other local groups. This is a tremendous disservice to everyone. A coven is not a "do it by the numbers" game; it's an extended family, and its formation should be treated accordingly. Seriously consider a trial period for all prospective members of your group—a time during which either you or they can back out of the relationship with no hard feelings. This trial period saves a lot of potential future problems.

Beyond this, all the considerations for a study group apply here, with the minor exception that you'll be determining the tradition to follow and the focus of rituals and spells rather than specific study topics. A coven often does gather to study their tradition together, but this is a completely different activity than that of the magic circle. It's usually too time-consuming and draining to combine the two goals, so hold your group studies at a separate time.

Once a core group is established, the leader needs to remain very aware of each member's outlooks, needs, and goals. Priests and Priestesses are not dictators who randomly mete out decisions or orders. They're helpmates and guides. For your coven to remain harmonious, there has to be some type of democracy and ample opportunities for everyone to voice opinions (especially with regard to someone petitioning for membership). A leader can still veto things, with good reason but an explanation to go along with the veto will definitely help maintain respect and cooperative attitudes.

I should note at this point that it's not a necessity that an elder or an adept lead, or even participate in, a coven. Covens offer fellowship, the power that comes from collective creation, and an opportunity to celebrate our tradition with others of a like mind but they're not right for everyone. Many people, like me, choose a solitary practice in which they teach one on one as opportunities arise.

If you find your path has but one set of footprints, don't berate yourself or try and fit into an uncomfortable role because others might wish it. One of the great signs of adepthood is knowing who you are as a spiritual being, and what you can (or cannot) do from this perspective. If groupwork isn't right for you, if leadership isn't a role that you've been called to, then just say so. People may not understand immediately, and some will be disappointed, but you are doing the right thing. Trust your heart.

HEALING

During the Middle Ages (and many other eras), it was common to find the village wise person dispensing magical remedials for everything from a case of the sniffles or restoring a cow's milk to replenishing barren land. In reviewing the recommendations of these healers, some prescriptions seem silly, others odd, and others still completely incomprehensible. Yet it is from the same historical resources that we come by the reborn art of herbalism as well as many of our modern treatment sequences. For example, healers once recommended toad skin as a curative for patients with heart problems. Now we know that this skin contains a (toxic) chemical similar to the heart medication digoxin!

With this rich and interesting legacy in mind, reaching out to people, animals, plants, or Earth itself with positive thought, skill, and healing energy is definitely a service suited to the Adept's Path. Exactly what form the healing takes depends much upon your gifts and holistic knowledge. Thanks to the New Age emphasis on the body-mind-spirit connection and reciprocity with nature, the world of holistic and alternative medicine is filled with magical overtones that an adept can apply in serving the community.

One adept may blend magical and medicinal herbalism techniques together to make empowered teas or lotions. Another individual might learn auric cleansing and balancing, or how to create health amulets. Another still could work Earth healing spells, use acupressure during a waning moon to encourage "shrinking" pain, or teach people metaphysical color therapy. Other healing traditions that work well with metaphysical ideology include but are not limited to:

- Aromatherapy
- Sound therapy
- Jin Shin Do
- Elemental work
- Bach flowers
- Acupuncture
- Homeopathy
- Therapeutic touch
- Polarity therapy
- Meditation
- Reiki
- Crystals
- Bodywork
- Massage
- Hypnosis

In considering healing as a potential service, remember that some healing arts require study and practice to learn, while others require only mental focus and good intentions. No matter the approach or methodology you settle upon, always work with a loving heart and empathetic ears. Like many other methods in advanced Witchcraft, healing has numerous facets and degrees, many of which are beautifully simple. Sometimes all people need to feel better is someone who listens and really cares. Sometimes all your corner of Earth needs is someone who lives eco-consciously. Any gesture toward these ends is a worthy service that leaves behind the gifts of compassion and hope—two types of magic whose powers should not be underestimated.

COUNSELING

No matter the era or culture, nearly every wise person ever born has taken on the role of counselor. While preparing an herbal mixture for fertility, for example, a village healer might gently give a nervous young bride some insights into married life. Or when concocting a love potion, the magus might give the purchaser hints on where to look for a suitable mate. All in all, the comfort and hope such people provided were just as important as their magic. This remains true today.

Within and without our communities, people are always seeking sound advice (whether they listen to it or not is another matter). As spiritual beings walking the Adept's Path, it is our charge to help whenever and wherever we can. This does not mean setting yourself up as an "expert" in everything and spouting off at every opportunity—it simply means sharing insights in situations where you feel you have something valid to offer. It means remaining alert and attentive to those who might be seeking someone to just listen unconditionally. It means wisely knowing when to speak and when to remain silent.

To fulfill the role of counselor, different people take different approaches. Some, like myself, accept the role of the proverbial mother to everyone who crosses the threshold. I must admit that it's odd sometimes to be called "Mom" by people my own age but it's a term of honor and respect to me. The folks who call me by this title are friends whom I've taken under wing and helped through difficult situations, ranging from sickness and death to a broken heart.

A second counseling role is that of the diviner. Here, instead of directly offering advice, the adept uses a tool that provides insights to the seeker. The tool is important to the counseling process for many reasons. It:

- Offers unique perspectives from the universe that the adept may not perceive-without assistance.
- Provides unbiased information (adepts are not immune to personal opinion and incorrect assumptions).
- Allows seekers to keep very private matters unspoken and still get answers.
- Gives seekers something to focus their attention on other than the counselor. This provides a modicum of emotional distance and puts the seekers' responsibility for their lives firmly in their own hands.
- Allows, in some instances, seekers to get directly involved in the reading by pulling cards or throwing stones (for example). This mingles seekers' auric energy with the tool and provides more specific, timely answers (even to questions that have remained unasked!).

If you choose to use divination as a tool for counseling others, bear in mind that there are some general rules that an ethical diviner follows. First, and most important, stress that a reading only reveals *possible* futures. Every moment of living changes our tomorrows, so the seeker can transform a bad scenario into something more productive just by remaining consciously aware and active.

Second, no matter what the reading portrays, try to find constructive, positive ways to phrase bad news. No one should leave a session feeling pessimistic or discouraged. This negative energy will draw more of the same to seekers and become their undoing. On the other hand, a good dose of hope can work wonders toward making a change for the better.

Third, don't allow seekers to use divination as a crutch. A diviner's services should be sought when personal perspective seems lacking, but individuals still must decide what to do with the information received. So, never phrase your readings in terms like, "you must...." Instead, use phrases like, "it might be worth considering...." This approach returns seekers to the altar of their own heart in determining how to proceed from this moment forward.

Finally, encourage seekers to ask questions about symbols that they don't understand for clarification. By taking time to answer these queries, you indirectly teach seekers about divination tools and archetypes. You also provide them with an invaluable opportunity to integrate the information they've just received.

An even more subtle way of counseling is through networking. Here, instead of offering advice directly, you give individuals personally known, trustworthy resources for whatever it is they seek. In the magical community, this is one of our most powerful tools. I've seen calls for assistance and various warnings reach coast to coast within hours thanks to our strong networking ties.

Networking offers many advantages. First, it gives you a way to direct people toward other skilled adepts in fields where your knowledge may be lacking or incomplete. Second, it allows you to choose sources that you can trust with seekers' spiritual welfare in redirecting them. Third, it keeps you in touch with what's happening in the Witchcraft community on a global basis. Along the same lines, networking stresses the community as a cooperative environment in which we support and promote those with verifiable training and knowledge, and those who practice honestly, with proper intention.

MONITORING AND REGULATION

This is perhaps the most important and difficult task of adepts and elders. Given the Witch wars and other disruptions facing the modem magical movement, we often are our own worst enemies. There are certain universal guidelines that all magic, and all life, works within. When someone tries to blur these lines or step over them altogether, it's spiritually harmful not only to that individual but to the network of magic itself. The task of an elder and an adept is that of taking such problems in hand and dealing with them diplomatically and firmly.

There is absolutely nothing manipulative or "unspiritual" about calling a spade a spade. Remember: those within our communities who are in it just for the money, are on ego trips, are using magic for ill ends, or claim to have training or knowledge that they do not possess are the very people whom the media loves to focus on. These are the individuals who give magic a bad name and keep us anchored in the old stereotypes.

I have grown very weary of purported "leaders" who pussyfoot around these issues—issues that threaten to tear apart the very fibers of our faith and our communities. Worse yet, there are people who choose to ignore the issues altogether. If you are walking the Adept's Path, you must leave apathetic attitudes behind you and become proactive here and now. Nothing less than a positive, mainstream future for the Craft is at stake.

Before trying to clean up our acts from the inside out, however, there are some good guidelines to follow in your efforts:

- Don't speak or act based on unsubstantiated gossip. Get your facts straight and go to the source before jumping on the condemnation bandwagon. Facts are your armor in the proverbial lion's den.

- Remember that there are two (or more) sides to every story. Try to hear all of them before coming to a conclusion and creating a plan of action.
- Some situations, no matter how volatile, are none of your business (like the interactions between a parent and a child). If the situation really bothers you or affects you somehow, talk over your concerns with someone who is already involved, then step back and let this person handle it.
- When you find yourself in the middle of a compromising or inappropriate situation, graciously retreat. Look for an unbiased party more suited to troubleshooting in this scenario.
- Similarly, try to stay away from mediating in situations where you cannot put aside personal experience or bias. The hope of doing our housecleaning is to bring everything back into balance. Any intense related history or biases can taint your capacity to treat people or a situation objectively. Know when to bow out.
- Even with all the facts in hand, you can still come to an incorrect or inaccurate conclusion, offer the wrong advice, or misjudge someone altogether. When you screw up, admit it, apologize, and fix any damage you've done. This is called *culpability*, and people will respect your honesty.
- Bearing the last point in mind, be discreet in your investigations and approach. As the old saying goes, a bull in a china shop is going to break or damage something. Ours is to heal, not to harm.
- Give people or groups the opportunity to right wrongs. If they choose not to, or simply ignore the chance, this says much in itself. But by offering that opportunity, you put the responsibility for action or inaction where it belongs.

- Don't always try to be the lone warrior. Find other adepts or elders in the community who are aware of the situation and seek their advice or aid. The more positive voices you can add to your own, the greater the overall impact of the intervention. Also, you cannot carry the burdens of the whole magical community on your shoulders and hope to function effectively.
- Unless it's a matter of mundane law that requires your direct testimony, keep confidences safe when resolving a problem. As an elder Priest, or Priestess, you have a duty to honor the trust people place in you and protect this trust.
- Finally, bear in mind that people are people. Everyone's going to make mistakes along their magical paths. Every group's going to have internal problems. And in every era of spiritual awakening, there will be those who abuse people's thirst for real experiences and profit from the trend. This is just human nature. We can't fix everything all at once, but we can make magic better through one person or one situation at a time. This is our task as adepts: to be the best role models we can and encourage others to follow suit.

COMMUNITY MAGIC

In our pursuit of community service, one of the greatest gifts we can give to each of our communities is our magic. Whether it's magic we perform specifically for a community or the magic we create with a community, the result is positive energy. This energy holds the community together, keeps it safe, inspires unity, generates improved communication, and makes you an important part of the entire picture.

So, as you go about your daily rituals, light candles and weave spells for all the communities in your life (family, friends, town, state, and so on). Say a prayer that they stay healthy, happy, and moving ever toward the light. Enact rituals that encourage tolerance, respect, and kindness. And when you gather with other Witches, put some of your communal energy to work for similar causes. Ask the God or Goddess to watch among you and to guide your collective magic in serving the communities in which you abide, healing wounds, meeting needs, and blessing everyone and everything with sacred power. In the following section, you'll find one sample ritual for community welfare.

Solitary Community Ritual

Timing: Really anytime you feel the community in question needs a boost. Alternatively, consider waxing moons for growing cooperation or waning moons to decrease tensions. Perform the ritual by sunlight if the community needs clear, logical thought to overcome a problem, or by moonlight for improved intuitive senses.

Preparations: Try to gather small items that can represent the people of the community for whom you're performing this ritual. For example, when doing a ritual for your family, gather from each member one personal token that won't be missed, like a pen or barrette. (It's best to ask permission to work magic for anyone, but you can get symbolic items for each individual and release the magic in such a way that it indicates "acceptance by free will" or something similar.) Don't forget to include one to represent yourself! Alternatively, find an old puzzle and write the names of each person on the back of the cardboard. Break apart the puzzle and put it in a basket on the altar.

The Altar: A lit candle to represent Spirit's presence at the center point, a white ribbon long enough to wrap around your tokens or puzzle three times to the left, and the basket of items or puzzle pieces (and glue) to the right.

The Circle: At the North, have some soil and a seed (separated). At the East, have a hand fan. At the South, have a blend of sage and lavender incense burning to inspire peace and wisdom. At the West, have a libation of sweet wine.

The Invocation:

> *East: (Pick up the fan and hold it.)* "Powers of the East, I welcome you to this sacred space. Bear tolerance and understanding on each breeze and each breath I take. Bring my community together in harmony."

> *South: (Use the fan to disperse the smoke.)* "Powers of the South, I welcome you to this sacred space. Burn with my community's heart as the light of peace, truth, and wisdom." *(Leave the fan at this quarter point to free up your hands.)*

> *West: (Slowly pour out the wine as you speak. If you're working indoors, pour it into another container and take it outside later.)* "Powers of the West, I welcome you to this sacred space. Let your sweet insight flow throughout my community and bring healing."

> *North: (Place the seed in the soil as you speak.)* "Powers of the North, I welcome you to this sacred space. Let this seed represent a new beginning for my community— one rooted in beauty and bound by magic. So be it."

Activity: Go to the altar and place your hand over the basket of items or puzzle pieces. Visualize them being filled with light in every color in the rainbow, a symbol of the hope for a better future. Bless the tokens, saying:

> *"Spirit in whom we all have beginning and from whom my magic flows, bless my community with your vision and unity Let these tokens represent our harmony and mutual purpose. (If a puzzle, assemble it now using glue along each piece.) As I bind these in white (wrap the tokens or puzzle with the ribbon), fill our spirits and hearts with positive intentions, kind words, and love."*

Closing: Dismiss the quarters in any manner you deem appropriate. Consider including a prayer to your god or goddess to empower the ritual's energy and guide it toward manifestation.

Keep the charm created during your ritual in a safe place afterward where it will not be disturbed or unwrapped. The only time you might want to dismantle the token is if someone is leaving the community represented. In such instances, gently open the token, release that individual with love and understanding, and then rebind the charm so that the community isn't disrupted by the changing energies.

As you give of your time and spiritual energy in rituals like this, the world around you cannot help but be affected. Transformations may be slow, but they will come. In your community, be it city, state, or even global, our magic will begin building the foundation for a better tomorrow.

SELF-CARE AND MAINTENANCE

As you begin the process of reaching out, I have some very important advice to share that comes from personal experience. Begin slowly and prudently, bearing in mind your other mundane responsibilities. The world is a very needy place. No one person can fill all its needs, no matter how much you might wish to love Earth and its people into wholeness. Just like anyone else's, an adept's body, mind, and spirit need regular care and maintenance.

Remember: everything you hope to accomplish cannot be done if the inner well is dry, if you are sick, you're out of sorts, or your energy is spread too thinly. So, serve with love but also serve wisely. Stop periodically and "just say no." Refill the well of self with the waters of spirit, then return to your communities refreshed.

To those of you who accept the Adept's Path and its sometimes-burdensome cloak, I wish you well. The adventure you're embarking upon is not easy, but it is a very worthy endeavor for yourself and all the lives your magic touches. To those of you already in service, this book is a personal thank-you card. Without your teaching, your patience, and your insights, my life (and many others) would not be the wondrous, magical place it is today. My prayers and good wishes are with you always. Blessed be.

AFTERWORD

THE DIVINE COPILOT

Not everyone approaches magic as a religious system. Some people use its methods as a way of directing the energy of the cosmos. I believe that the Path of the Adept, the path of advanced Wicca, leads us to the Divine Source whose spark ignited the big bang and continues energizing our magic.

The uninitiated are often befuddled by the myriad names by which we call this Parent. Zeus, Kwan Yin, Pele, Bacchus—these names are different aspects of the One. They reflect the diversity of humankind's characteristics, good and bad, light and dark, life and death. Any power so great must contain this variety so that we can recognize that originating spark in our hearts and keep it burning bright.

Adepts are the firekeepers and guardians of secrets. Every day they watch to make sure spiritual flames stay steady, never dying, and never raging out of control. They use this light to fight back the darkness and to stand watch diligently over the Ancient Ways. But this need not be a lone vigil.

We can call upon the Sacred to strengthen the spark within, shed light without, and help protect that which we hold dear. So, consider looking to the god/dess as a copilot on your personal spiritual sojourn. No matter what facet or name you relate to, allow this Being to inspire, hearten, energize, refine, and shine on your path every moment of every day.

RECOMMENDED READING

Recommending specific reading is difficult because there aren't many advanced books out, and because which books you read is going to depend a lot on your path and vision. These are some that I've found particularly helpful in writing this book:

Aldington, Richard, translator. New *Larousse Encyclopedia of Mythology*. Hamlyn Publishing, 1973.
Arrien, Angeles. The *Four Fold Way*. HarperCollins, 1993.
Beyerl, Paul. *Herbal Magick*. Phoenix Publishing, 1998.
Bruce-Mitford, Miranda. *The Illustrated Book of Signs & Symbols*. DK Publishing, 1996.
Budge, E. A. Wallis. *Amulets & Superstitions*. Oxford University Press, 1930.
Cavendish, Richard. A *History of Magic*. Taplinger Publishing, 1979.
Cooper, J. C. *Symbolic & Mythological Animals*. Aquarian Press, 1992.

Cunningham, Scott. *Crystal, Gem & Metal Magic.* Llewellyn Publications, 1995.

Davison, Michael Worth, editor. *Everyday Life Through the Ages.* Reader's Digest Association, Ltd., 1992.

Gordon, Leslie. *Green Magic.* Viking Press, 1977.

Gordon, Stuart. *Encyclopedia of Myths and Legends.* Headline Book Publishing, 1993.

Hall, Manly P. *Secret Teachings of All Ages.* Philosophical Research Society, 1977.

Hurley, J. Finley. *Sorcery.* Routledge & Kegan Paul, 1985.

Jordan, Michael. *Encyclopedia of Gods.* Facts on File, Inc., 1993.

Kieckhefer, Richard. *Magic in the Middle Ages.* Cambridge University Press, 1989.

Kowalchik, Claire, and William Hylton, editors. *Kodak's Illustrated Encyclopedia of Herbs.* Rodale Press, 1987.

Kunz, George Frederick. *Curious Lore of Precious Stones.* Dover Publications, 1971.

Leach, Maria, editor. *Standard Dictionary of Folklore, Mythology, and Legend.* Harper & Row, 1984.

Loewe, Michael, and Carmen Blacker, editors. *Oracles and Divination.* Shambhala, 1981.

Matthews, John, editor. *The World Atlas of Divination.* Bullfinch Press, 1992.

Miller, Gastavus Hindman. *Ten Thousand Dreams Interpreted.* M. A. Donohue & Co., 1931.

Sargent, Denny. *Global Ritualism.* Llewellyn Publications, 1994.

Spence, Lewis. *The Encyclopedia of the Occult.* Bracken Books, 1988.

Telesco, Patricia. *Futuretelling.* Crossing Press, 1997.

—. *The Herbal Arts.* Crossed Crow Books, 2024.

—. *The Language of Dreams.* Crossing Press, 1997.

—. *Spinning Spells, Weaving Wonders.* Crossed Crow Books, 2024.
—. *A Witch's Book of Ceremonies and Rituals.* Crossed Crow Books, 2025.
—. *Your Book of Shadows.* Crossed Crow Books, 2025.
Walker, Barbara. *The Woman's Dictionary of Symbols and Sacred Objects.* Harper & Row, 1988.